The Brain that Loves to Play

This delightful visual book provides an accessible introduction to how play affects the holistic development and brain growth of children from birth to five years. Written by a leading expert, it brings current theory to life by inviting the reader to celebrate the developing brain that loves to play and is hungry for sensitive human interaction and rich play opportunities.

Packed full of images and links to film clips of children playing in a variety of contexts on the companion website, chapters focus on different ages and stages of development, providing snapshots of real play scenarios to explore their play preferences and the theory that underpins their play behaviour. With clear explanations of what is happening in the body and brain at each "stage," this book reveals the richness of the play opportunities on offer and the adult's role in facilitating it. Each chapter follows an easy-to-navigate format which includes:

- Best practice boxes showing how play in different contexts has impacted a child's development
- QR codes linking to short film clips on a companion website to exemplify key points
- Brain and body facts sections providing short accessible explanations of key theories
- Play and pedagogy discussion questions
- Extended material to support the level four descriptors for degree-level study

With opportunities to dig deeper, full-colour photographs, and a fully integrated companion website, *The Brain that Loves to Play* is essential reading for all early years students and practitioners and all those with an interest in child development.

Jacqueline Harding is Director of Tomorrow's Child and Senior Lecturer at Middlesex University. She is an internationally acclaimed child development expert with experience as a BBC education editor, Headteacher, government consultant, and author of numerous books for and about children. Jacqueline also works in children's TV production.

The Brain that Loves to Play

A Visual Guide to Child Development, Play, and Brain Growth

JACQUELINE HARDING

Routledge
Taylor & Francis Group

LONDON AND NEW YORK

Designed cover image: © Getty Images

First published 2024
by Routledge
4 Park Square, Milton Park, Abingdon, Oxon, OX14 4RN

and by Routledge
605 Third Avenue, New York, NY 10158

Routledge is an imprint of the Taylor & Francis Group, an informa business

British Library Cataloguing-in-Publication Data
A catalogue record for this book is available from the British Library

Library of Congress Cataloging-in-Publication Data
Names: Harding, Jacqueline, 1958- author.
Title: The brain that loves to play : a visual guide to child development,
    play and brain growth / Jacqueline Harding.
Description: First edition. | Abingdon, Oxon ; New York, NY : Routledge, 2023. |
    Includes bibliographical references and index. |
Identifiers: LCCN 2023006922 (print) | LCCN 2023006923 (ebook) |
    ISBN 9781032314402 (hardback) | ISBN 9781032314396 (paperback) |
    ISBN 9781003309758 (ebook)
Subjects: LCSH: Play--Psychological aspects. | Child development.
Classification: LCC BF717 .H256 2023 (print) | LCC BF717 (ebook) |
    DDC 155.4/18--dc23/eng/20230623
LC record available at https://lccn.loc.gov/2023006922
LC ebook record available at https://lccn.loc.gov/2023006923

ISBN: 978-1-032-31440-2 (hbk)
ISBN: 978-1-032-31439-6 (pbk)
ISBN: 978-1-003-30975-8 (ebk)

DOI: 10.4324/9781003309758

Typeset in Folio
by KnowledgeWorks Global Ltd.

Printed in the UK by Severn, Gloucester on responsibly sourced paper

Access the Instructor and Student Resources: www.routledge.com/cw/Harding

Dedication:

This book is dedicated to my husband Colin, sister Debbie, and mother – all of whose patience and belief in me is never-ending. And, to my four children: Sam, Holly, Mark, and Pete and all nine fantastic grandchildren: … you taught me everything I needed to know.

Contents

Foreword

Dr Dimitri A. Christakis is the director of the Center for Child Health, Behavior and Development at Seattle Children's Research Institute. He is a paediatrician at Seattle Children's Hospital in Seattle and a professor in the School of Medicine at the University of Washington. He is also Chair of the Bright Start Foundation.

At the Bright Start Foundation, we believe that every child deserves the very best start in life and this book highlights the many delightful ways in which that can be achieved.

I am personally committed to the belief that "If you change the beginning, you change the whole story" and I am delighted to see how theory is brought to life in this unique and compelling book. The combination of films and photographs together with clear explanations of the way in which children develop makes this a "must-have" book for every practitioner, student, and parent.

This book will change your thinking about how young children learn and put a spring in your step as you support children on their developmental journey.

Professor Dimitri Christakis

Welcome to the world of play where the brain gets to do what it loves best … to play with absolute abandon!

Acknowledgements

Lourdes Kerr: I am truly indebted to Lourdes for her unending support, commitment, and enthusiasm for this book throughout the whole process and granting me permission to write about her nursery and the amazing children who play there!

Katie Madgett: I am so grateful to Katie for fact checking and her in-depth knowledge of child development as a midwife and health visitor.

Natasha Cobby RN BSc HEDip Advanced Clinical Practitioner Trainee and *Dr Marc Rayan*: I am truly thankful to you both for fact checking the brain growth and anatomy sections of this book.

Colin Vallance: I wholeheartedly thank Colin for his proofreading and initial editing.

Alina Ursuleanu: I am indebted to Alina for her immense help in reading the manuscript and making valuable comments and suggestions.

Naomi Wildsmith: I am so grateful for the fact that you are not only a knowledgeable play therapist but also an enthusiastic contributor to this book in so many ways.

Fisher Price: I am indebted to Fisher Price, who in 2020 commissioned me to explore the possible benefits of parent/carers involvement in object play with their children (under three years of age) with a specific focus on what the adult may or may not gain from the experience.

Judy Dick: I am so thankful to Judy for her grounded understanding of young children and enthusiasm to help with this book.

Samuel Harding: As always, I am impressed by the quality of Samuel's work as a photographer – capturing the true essence of play for children. Many thanks also to Zaine Zeini for his photographic contributions to this book.

Emelie Rennella: I am grateful to Emelie for the two amazing photographs of Holly and Quinn, and of course little Janos who brings much laughter to this book.

All researchers and professionals featured in this book: I am humbled by your generosity of time; I could not have written this book without your expertise.

Parents and practitioners: My sincere thanks for your generosity and kindness in allowing me to write about your children and for giving me permission to use their precious films and images in this book.

acknowledgements

Janos and his dad

Introduction

In this video (mentioned in Figure 0.1, accessible via the QR code), I share with you the motivation for writing this book and my passion for play and its benefits to all-round development.

Ethan jumps wholeheartedly into a puddle: total physical abandonment with arms outstretched, face tilted towards the rain, and a broad smile reaching across his face. At this very moment, his brain also starts to "jump" and light up with joy as connections between neurons make impressive progress. Does this experience count as learning? Absolutely yes. The architecture of the brain

Figure 0.1 Jacqueline. See video "Jacqueline speaks about the book" via the QR code

DOI: 10.4324/9781003309758-1

Figures 0.2 The joy of jumping in puddles!

wallowing in the sensory experience forms new neural pathways' which in turn unlock opportunities for more formal learning. Do most theorists today agree that play is vital and important? Yes, but is it more widely known as the most *efficient* way to make educational progress in the early years? Probably not. These neural play-driven pathways laid down before the age of six years have the most profound impact on future opportunities and must not be ignored. It seems that the young child's body and brain is literally designed to be playful, and this is crucial for its development. Of course, children should play for the sake of playing. Children are naturally wired to play and any sustained deviation from this masterful design comes at a price. For the young child, the scene is set for them to fully embrace the learning on offer through rich sensory playful experiences and it is an opportunity that neither body nor brain can afford to abandon.

With a renewed vision for the fusion of "play" and "learning," this book intends to contribute to the ongoing discussion for redefining the way we care, educate, and parent young children. It is not intended to be an exhaustive catalogue of all that has happened in neuroscience, play, or in child development over the last 20 years, but it does offer a window into this emerging field and attempts to demonstrate just how we can all make a difference to children by fully embracing both theory and practice.

LIGHTING UP THE BRAIN THAT LOVES TO PLAY

We might not have all the answers about how the brain works yet but we do know enough to say that play is an integral part of nurturing it. Play is efficient and its impact long-lasting. There is no doubt, according to all the latest research (which we will dip into throughout this book), that the brain loves to play, and it is time that adults (students, practitioners, and parents) get on board with this notion too.

Any historical division between play and learning needs to be challenged and the application of new research into brain science is an area that is yet to be fully explored. But perhaps because it appears too difficult to join the dots, is too obvious or is simply hidden in plain sight, it is generally overlooked. And yet, it is well established that the affordances of play do not stop at the gate of learning – they travel even further into the territory of health and well-being. Professor Robert Winston (2016:12) is convinced that "Infancy is a crucial time for brain development." The early years is the perfect time to focus on activities that support brain growth. The child's body and brain derive such enduring benefits from play that both educational, mental health researchers and physicians are beginning to value its inherent properties as never before. New government initiatives, such as Social Prescribing, also acknowledge the source of play as a powerful way forward for health and well-being for adults. Play must not stop as we grow older because its value to our own health and well-being is profound and is confirmed by numerous researchers, such as Brown and Vaughan (2009), whose work bears testimony to its effectiveness.

Why this book was written

The book was written in order to offer fresh approaches to tired debates about "play" for children, grounded in wide, cross-disciplinary literature reviews. I truly believe that the basics of the science behind play and child development is well within the understanding of most interested adults – students, practitioners, and parents. The divide between "the professional with expert knowledge" and the recipient of knowledge must be eroded if research is to be beneficial to babies and children in our care. As Conkbayir (2021) points out, neuroscience offers undeniable insights for practitioners, but for several unhelpful reasons, such as cynicism from various quarters, lack of accurate information (myths), or media hype, the safe practical implications of new knowledge rarely make their way into current practice.

The viewpoint of the child

The meaningful questions that adults, parents, and practitioners have asked me over the years reveal their strong motivation to fully understand brain development. They *care* about the well-being of babies and children and truly wish to understand the viewpoint of the child: how they think, what life *looks like* from their point of view. Play is an impressive vehicle for development, so it is important to demystify some of the terminology and understanding around it and to explain what healthy brain and body development really means. The intention is not for us all to pretend that we know more than we do (although a little knowledge may not always be a "bad thing"), as at the heart of the book is a passion for a more joyful and less serious early years' experience for *all* children and the adults around them.

What might you gain from this book?

The book's practical approach aims to make compelling reading for those who wish to move seamlessly between theory and practice while not degrading academic credibility.

What is the main message?

The emphasis in this book is firmly on why the brain loves to play and the developmental benefits of playful experiences and human interaction. It is not an instructional handbook on how to plan educational programmes. A fusion of play and learning is a balanced place for any application of play pedagogy and understanding of holistic child development. Internationally, there is mounting concern for children's well-being (Nelson et al., 2020). Recent urgent discussions have centred around assessing children's mental health in the wake of the pandemic and the subject of play is at the forefront of some solution-focussed discussions. *Early intervention, also known as early help,* means identifying and providing the precise support to a family as soon as possible when a problem arises. The evidence around the long-term impact of the pandemic on children's mental health and how to provide early intervention through boosting collaboration between service providers, local authorities, and parents is an important issue (Best Beginnings, Home-Start UK, 2020).

Practitioners and those studying early childhood on a variety of courses now encounter the need to revisit and re-evaluate how play impacts the all-round development and brain growth of children from birth to five years.

So who might benefit from the contents of this book?

This book is written for those who wish to better understand the value of play to the developing child and how brain development can be sensitively nurtured while avoiding the common pitfalls of misinterpreting emerging brain science. You may be a practitioner, student, teacher, and researcher from a range of disciplines, such as early years education, child development, social sciences, or an undergraduate studying similar courses. Real-life case studies accompanied by stimulating "discussion starters" later on in the text also offer a ready-made resource for busy lecturers and training providers.

Importantly, this book also aims to empower those who are pregnant with their first child, parents, grandparents, and kinship carers, who often feel excluded from such discussions and who wish to embrace the fusion of play and learning into their everyday care for young children. It is my belief that a greater awareness of how we can support children is vital for *all* who care for young children. In these changeable times, as we emerge from a pandemic which has significantly impacted all our lives, there can be no better place to begin than considering how we can rewrite the narrative through support in the early years.

Changing the story

In 2020, Dr Dimitri Christakis, director of the Center for Child Health, Behavior and Development, wrote about the impact of COVID on young children in the journal *Pediatrics and COVID-19*. He describes some of the most profound effects on children's psychological and educational well-being. He cites concerns regarding adverse effects on attachment and breastfeeding for newborn babies separated briefly from their mothers at birth because of concern for vertical transmission. Furthermore, he expresses dismay for the numerous children who were raised by parents who experienced (and are continuing to experience) financial and psychological stress because of the pandemic. Dr Christakis highlights research that demonstrates how parental stress has been shown to be associated with changes in cortisol regulation as well as brain structure and function in children and young adults. The mantra of his lab is: "If you change the beginning you change the whole story." He is deeply concerned that the pandemic has assuredly changed the beginning for millions of children.

Figure 0.3 Trudy. See video "Trudy Darien speaks about mental health and 'getting it right' in the early years" via the QR code

Do take a look at this important film clip (mentioned in Figure 0.3, accessible via the QR code), where Trudy Darien, an organisational Psychotherapist, shares her substantial experience in this field and relates theory to practice. Note how she echoes Dr Christakis' call to change the beginning and effect change for life.

Visual representations

Vivid written descriptions of real children at play, together with spontaneously filmed footage and images, capture the essence of play *in that moment* for the child or children and help to make valuable highly complex theory relating to play and brain development, totally accessible.

It is my hope that these genuine personal filmed vignettes, together with photographs of young children's play behaviours, will be immediately recognisable and will provide a surprising depth of visual data to study and consider. This bite-sized visual model is offered as an effective and accessible way of recalling developmental progress and sensory-based activities, which will act as a suitable reminder on which to build other reference points. For example, in later practice, you may be working with a child who masters a skill in an unexpected way. This "visual picture"

Figure 0.4 Child laughing

can be added to the repertoire of what you know about how different children achieve skills in a variety of ways. And, when these real-life moments are explained in the light of the work of theorists, the understanding of play and learning is strengthened for you, the reader. Therefore, as a starting point, the content draws on lived play experiences for young children as told by parents/carers/practitioners and children themselves. The content, which is intentionally not professionally filmed but more "fly on the wall" and left unedited, avoids any performance on the part of the child or adult and ensures that the viewer's attention is drawn to the general development and brain growth opportunities on offer. This is all interwoven with essential play theory and is underpinned by relevant safeguarding and welfare requirements, sound Early Years Foundation Stage (EYFS) planning, and attention to Special Educational Needs and Disabilities (SEND).

How to use this book

Rather than the usual structure of examining play theory and pedagogy with fleeting reference to the reality of what it might mean to the overall development of the child and the brain's neural connections, the starting point for this book is the focus on the child's developmental stage. It then moves on to examine how play impacts brain and body growth and addresses further play opportunities.

Figure 0.5 The keys to unlock the potential of the book

Unlocking the treasure

The first few chapters provide three essential keys to unlocking the rest of the book: child develop-ment, brain development, and play theory. With these keys in your hand, you are equipped to unlock the treasure trove of insights relating to the individual stages of development in later chapters.

Chapters 4–14 employ a rhythm which will swiftly become familiar. Each chapter begins by featuring children in case study filmed format so the reader will "get to know" the child/children and the adults who support them through a short film clip. A further short film clip may then follow, featuring an adult who may explain the scenario or provide further theoretical insight. The text also provides an understanding of the play and the theory that underpins the premise. An explanation of what is happening in the body and brain at any "stage" is also offered – making the theory "real" to the reader. Of course, every child is different, and the way children play and develop will have its own unique pathway. The reader is always encouraged to be sensitive and to consider issues such as gender, skin colour, types of hair, special needs, and disabilities, as well as religion in each activity. Importantly, there is an assumption that the reader will respect any child and family who may have English as a second language or have a disability, and that they have an equal right to the play described. Some children are particularly sensitive to sensory stimulation and care must be taken not to overstimulate at any point in their lives. So, please be aware that for the sake of the flow of the text, these points will never be overly highlighted.

How to use the QR codes

The short description under the QR codes describes the content of the film. There are a variety of films. For example:

- Films of children playing in a variety of ways
- Films of the views of the adult who provided or was involved in the play experience
- Films providing research interpretation of the play
- Films of experts in their field offering research-based evidence around particular areas

Each of these chapters draws on bite-sized films to set the scene for deeper discussions alongside complex pedagogy explained in everyday language.

Here are just a few of the children and their parents you will meet:

Among the many families, we especially follow Holly and Janos during his first two years of life:

Figure 0.6 Holly and Janos walk by the sea: Janos and his mum, Holly

Figure 0.7 Ethan and Levi play together: Ethan and Levi are brothers

Ethan and his older brother Levi, who also welcome another new baby into their lives.

We meet Lourdes and the children at her nursery and see how they embrace a range of creative play opportunities.

Figure 0.8 Lourdes and the children at her nursery

Figure 0.9 Naomi

Several experts comment on the film clips and provide their perspective on what is happening. Naomi is a play therapist.

Terms

For ease of reading, I have frequently chosen to use she/her when discussing children in general.

How to use the boxes

The text "boxes" in each chapter are described below.

- ☐ **The Best Practice** sections contain text relating to real-life examples of how play in its variety of contexts has impacted children's development.
- ☐ **The Brain and Body Sensory Development Pointers** sections provide bite-sized text and address how the developing brain and body are impacted by the sensory play activities investigated in that chapter.

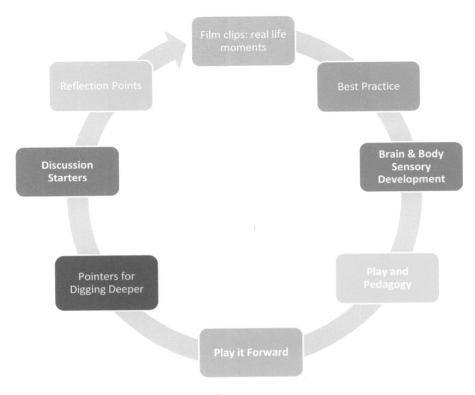

Figure 0.10 Navigating the material in the book

☐ **The Play and Pedagogy** sections provide theory which is explained and used as a stimulus for further discussion.

☐ **The Play it Forward sections** provide suggestions for practical, playful, sensory-based activities to build on the development at each stage.

☐ **The Pointers for Digging Deeper** sections offer extended material to nudge towards the level four descriptors for degree-level study and beyond. **Discussion Starters** are also offered.

☐ The **Reflection Points** sections offer final thoughts and a summary of main points from the chapter.

Accessing the material

You may wish to watch the films first via the QR codes and then pause before considering how research might interpret the play behaviour. Alternatively, the text and films can be searched via types of play or through specific developmental areas or even particular experiences. The "boxes" are provided as ways of exploring specifically identified areas relating to the chapter.

Although the following areas of play are evenly addressed throughout the book, this chart highlights where a particular area of play is featured. Of course, the relationship of play to brain development is embedded in each chapter and film.

Play and area of interest	Text in book	To be viewed on film or in photographs
	Chapter(s)	Chapter(s)
Adult play	3, 16	16
Block play	10	10
Combatting stress	16	16
Comfort	4, 8, 10, 12	8, 10, 12
Creativity	2, 3, 5, 7, 10, 12, 14, 15, 16	2, 10, 13, 14, 15, 16
Digital play	3, 14	14
Imagination	3, 8, 10, 11, 12, 14, 15	11, 12, 13, 15
Role-play	3, 11, 15	11, 13, 15
Language and play	5, 7, 9, 10, 11, 12, 13, 15	5, 7, 9, 10, 11, 13, 15
Laughter	3, 5, 10, 16	5, 8, 10, 16
Object play	3, 7, 8, 11, 12, 13	7, 8
Outdoor play	3, 8, 9, 10, 14, 15	8, 9, 10, 14, 15
Physical play	4, 8, 9, 14	4, 8, 9, 14
Role of adult	3, 5, 8, 10, 11, 12, 13, 14, 15, 16	3, 5, 10, 11, 13, 14, 15
Schemas	3, 9, 11, 15	11, 15
Social and emotional play and mental health	3, 4, 5, 6, 7, 8, 9, 10, 12, 13	3, 4, 5, 6, 7, 8, 10
Stages of play	3	3
The environment	3, 11	11, 13

Terminology and conventions

The importance of understanding that every child is unique and will follow their developmental journey differently cannot be over-emphasised. This book is solidly built on the enduring principles of equality of opportunity, ethnicity, race, gender, socio-economic status, family context, and inclusivity, and trusts that the reader will keep these important factors in mind when considering play activities.

Children's rights

Children are entitled to provision which enables them to develop their personalities, talents, and abilities irrespective of ethnicity, culture or religion, home language, family background, learning difficulties, disabilities, or gender as confirmed by *The United Nations Convention on the Rights of the Child* (1989). An in-depth knowledge of how children develop and a basic understanding of brain development and its relationship to the benefits of play is the best starting point to ensure that these entitlements become a reality.

Early Years Foundation Stage

The Department for Education (DfE) updated the EYFS framework in 2021. It sets the standards to ensure that children aged from birth to five years learn and develop well and are kept healthy and safe. This essential document helps practitioners design and prepare for activities and experiences that benefit the all-round development of children. The theories of play, together with an overview of how the brain develops communicated in this book, aim to compliment the DfE (2021) Early Years Foundation Framework. The suggested *Play it Forward* activities reflect the importance of all three prime areas, which are communication and language, physical development, and personal, social and emotional development, and the four specific areas, which are literacy, maths, understanding the world, and expressive arts and design.

Development matters

The *Brain and Body Sensory Development Pointers* contained in each chapter can be a useful companion to the DfE's (2021) document *Development Matters*, which is the non-statutory curriculum guidance for the early year's foundation stage. It is essential reading for a deeper understanding of ways in which to encourage the development explained in the following chapters.

1 Understanding the developing child

This chapter will introduce you to:
- The multiple areas of development
- Why it is important to support children in their all-round development
- Early intervention
- Inclusive practice
- Safeguarding issues
- Why observing children can be supportive

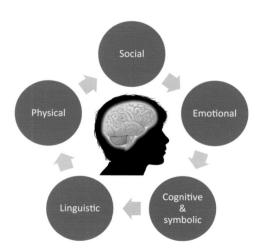

Figure 1.1 Interlocking areas of development

DOI: 10.4324/9781003309758-2

UNDERSTANDING THE MEANING OF CHILD DEVELOPMENT

Frequently, in textbooks, areas of development are described separately and this is simply for ease of understanding. Of course, child development is far from simple and the way in which each area of development interlocks with other areas of development is highly sophisticated. However challenging it may be to truly understand this complexity, we must try. The developing child *must* be seen holistically if adults are to avoid unnecessary misunderstandings and anxieties. For this reason, vocabulary used to describe behaviours or age ranges is chosen to reflect this holistic view.

There is, however, no doubt that precise descriptions associated with developmental trajectories are useful when used carefully and sensitively. Therefore, the wording and phrases chosen in this book, such as children usually start to demonstrate a skill "around or approaching …" a particular age, reflect a typical range of development within that age bracket. This is in recognition of the fact that some babies and children will take longer to achieve those next steps along their unique developmental path.

Early intervention

There is now general acceptance and agreement that acquiring knowledge of how children develop helps students, practitioners, and parents identify a child who might be encountering developmental difficulties. Observing a child playing is an excellent way of understanding their progress as well as identifying any possible delays. Most importantly, addressing any concerns early is often critical to future progress. Children benefit from early intervention through carefully planned play activities.

> *Research into adverse childhood experiences (ACEs) has generated a powerful and accessible narrative which has helpfully increased awareness of the lifetime impact of early adversity on children's outcomes,*

(Asmussen et al. 2020:10)

A balanced approach

Some applied knowledge of the basics of brain development and developmental theories is deeply interesting to read but it is the actual application of the theory to practice through playful activities that will truly make the difference to children. Of course, avoiding the inevitable pitfalls of popular myths about the brain or misappropriating the information is critical. A balanced approach safeguards children. Any new knowledge must be tested against what is evidenced-based and meets stringent safeguarding policies.

Figure 1.2 The child's needs are paramount. Sienna's nursery nurse Alma knows that individual attention for every child is essential

As a practitioner or parent, it's always a good idea to stand back and view the broader picture. This is the point at which observations of children in a variety of play situations at differing times, each with a specific developmental focus, can reveal more of what is truly happening. It builds a helpful comprehensive picture. Decisions that benefit the child can best be taken when with other professionals and parents/carers are all equipped with sufficient information.

Factors affecting overall development for both body and brain: It is important to consider many reasons that can aid or hinder growth and development. Here are just a few to consider:

- Access to high-quality play provision
- Work opportunities for parents

- Opportunities for children to play
- Income
- Housing
- Environmental factors
- Health status
- Genetics

The first two years

Strong evidence from around the world shows that the earliest years are extremely important. Research confirms that without consistent sensitive support, babies struggle to make the progress that is essential for human development. So, a thriving society itself depends on the fair treatment of its youngest citizens.

Figure 1.3 Babies need constant support right from birth to make the best progress. Baby Sunday enjoys exploring the world

Figure 1.4 Loving interaction can help build brains. Baby Grace is in receipt of consistent care and attention

Interestingly, human babies seem ill-equipped to survive when they enter the world. The actual extent of their underdevelopment is astounding. They are completely dependent on other humans for their very survival. For example, they are unable to be very mobile for several months and usually only take their first steps around the age of one. The human brain is significantly underdeveloped at birth, and it seems that appropriate sensory input alongside careful and loving interaction enables this truly complex organ to make its best progress. Children need to survive and thrive.

Building the brain

When it comes to the wiring of the brain – it isn't quite as straightforward as it might seem as some areas have priority in its architecture in the earliest years. Tierney and Nelson (2009:7) describe the higher level processes as being built on the lower level processes, and comment on the importance of sensory and perceptual development in this way: "The types of stimuli infants and children are exposed to help shape the brain and behaviour. Although the brain may come equipped with biases for certain perceptual information, such as for speech, language, or faces, it is the specific speech, language, and range of faces they are exposed to that drives subsequent development."

Developmentally speaking, so much importance seems to hang on those first two years. There are numerous published reports that have clarified the need for supportive action for families so that babies can make the best possible progress. Here are just a few:

- "First 1000 Days of Life," published by the House of Commons Health and Social Care Committee in February 2019. https://publications.parliament.uk/pa/cm201719/cmselect/cmhealth/1496/1496.pdf
- "Tackling Disadvantage in the Early Years," published by the House of Commons Education Committee in January 2019. https://publications.parliament.uk/pa/cm201719/cmselect/cmeduc/1006/1006.pdf
- "Best Beginnings in the Early Years," published by the former Children's Commissioner in July 2020. https://www.childrenscommissioner.gov.uk/report/best-beginnings-in-the-early-years/

Inclusive practice

Significant legislation in the UK supports inclusive education. Most recently, the UN Convention on the Rights of Persons with Disabilities is an important document to consider. https://www.un.org/development/desa/disabilities/convention-on-the-rights-of-persons-with-disabilities.html

The Equality Act (2010) clearly addresses the requirement that there must be no discrimination between pupils on grounds of race, sex, disability, sexual orientation, gender reassignment, pregnancy and maternity, religion or belief, in admissions, access to benefits or services, exclusions, or staff employment.

It is clearly established now that high-quality early education and care is inclusive. Children's special educational needs and disabilities (SEND) must be identified promptly.

Special educational needs and disability

The Children and Families Act (2014) ensures that local authorities have a statutory duty to provide services to parents and carers who have children with additional needs. Situations vary and so services need to be agile in their approach; sometimes the parents or carers will already be aware in pregnancy that their baby might have a disability and may experience developmental delays which affect their overall developmental progress. However, in other situations, this may take longer for a baby or child's actual needs to become assessed and identified. Multi-disciplinary care can provide support from a range of professionals in a coordinated way and there is consistent agreement that parents and carers welcome such an approach.

Early help

The first two years are often described as "the first 1,001 days" or the "Start for Life period" and are widely acknowledged as being a critical period for development, particularly in terms of communication, gross and fine motor skills, and physical skills. The policy paper "The best start for life: a vision for the 1,001 critical days" was published 25 March 2021, see: https://www.gov.uk/government/publications/the-best-start-for-life-a-vision-for-the-1001-critical-days

Early help (and that includes the perinatal period) works to ensure that all children receive the support and help they need to make good progress. At the heart of sound inclusive practice in the early years is the need for every child to feel a sense of belonging and to help all children develop positive attitudes towards diversity and inclusion. Inclusive play practice will always aim to minimise or remove barriers to high-quality play activities and experiences. As mentioned earlier, every child will develop at their own pace, so inclusive practice concerns paying attention to their individual backgrounds, interests, and needs. Obligations for practitioners in the Early Years Foundation Stage and the SEND Code of Practice are clear. Early intervention can make a world of difference to a child with additional needs and prepares them for a more positive experience of play and learning. The reader is trusted to ensure that the child's individual needs are embraced and play activities are inclusive.

Safeguarding children

Child protection is the process of protecting a child identified as suffering from, or potentially suffering from, significant harm as a result of abuse or neglect. *Working Together to Safeguard Children* (HM Government, 2018) is the latest government guidance. In essence, it means:

- Children must be protected from maltreatment
- Impairment of children's health or development must be prevented
- Children must be given the opportunity to grow up in circumstances consistent with the provision of safe and effective care
- Action must be taken to enable all children to achieve the best outcomes

There are key principles that underpin safeguarding, for example, a child's needs should be put first, and support provided as early as possible.

The Early Years Foundation Stage provides the foundation of safeguarding measures for early years' providers to follow and the government guidance. *Working Together to Safeguard Children* (HM Government, 2018) and *What to do if you are worried a child is being abused* (HM Government, 2015) provide a national framework to safeguard children.

Brief descriptions of each area of development

In the following chapters, as each case study is described, it is useful to keep in mind a basic overview of each area of development.

Personal, social, and emotional

Broadly, this area concerns:

- Development of a positive sense of self and others
- Formation of positive relationships
- Development of respect for others
- Development of social skills
- Management of feelings
- Understanding of appropriate behaviour in groups
- Confidence in own abilities

Physical development

Broadly, this area concerns:

- Development of coordination control and movement
- Gross motor skills (movements made by arms, legs, or entire body); these skills involve the large muscles of the body that enable, for example, running and throwing to develop
- Fine motor skills (the small movements of the body and use of the muscles that enable, for example, grasping small objects)

Communication and language

Broadly, this area concerns:

- Language development
- Development of confidence and skills in expression
- Ability to speak and listen in a range of situations

Cognitive and symbolic

Broadly, this area concerns:

- Development of understanding, analysis, and evaluation of concepts and the ability to make sense of the world

POINTERS FOR DIGGING DEEPER

Let's turn to watch the clip (mentioned in Figure 1.5, accessible via the QR code), where Professor Pat Preedy shares her insights about play and movement. She is passionate about early childhood education and over many years has led international research, contributing greatly to our knowledge and understanding of the development and needs of babies and young children.

Figure 1.5 Professor Preedy. See video "Get moving!" via the QR code

The Motor Movers programme for schools and nurseries is a range of specific exercises designed to be delivered to the whole class on a daily basis and is an initiative based on the foundations of the Movement for Learning Project. Professor Preedy and Laura Preedy-Maher developed this for teachers of young children to provide a neurodevelopment fine and gross motor skills programme. They believe that babies and children throughout the world go through the same stages of development (although there are several factors that impact if and when children reach these milestones) in order to get their bodies and minds ready for learning. Professor Preedy highlights key milestones such as control of the head, hands, and feet whilst on the back; rolling onto the tummy; gaining control of the head from a prone position; belly or commando crawling; crawling; full sitting; standing and walking.

Importance of movement

There is mounting concern about the recent trend of a reduction in time for physical activity, and an increase in screen time and the use of hand-held devices in modern life is impeding the physical development of many young children. Professor Preedy's work has shown that the impact of poor physical development is more wide-ranging than just affecting physical skills and the ability to participate in physical activities such as sports. A child who struggles with balance, gross, and fine motor skills is also likely to struggle with concentration, reading, writing, and personal skills such as doing up a coat or managing a knife and fork (Duncombe & Preedy, 2018).

Holistic approach

Being mindful of the way in which all the biological systems in the child's body are related helps us ensure that we take a holistic view of the benefits of play experiences that support the "whole child": this includes emotional and social competence, strengthening the building blocks of mental and physical health, and readiness for later learning. The "brain that loves to play" is a helpful way to view the nourishment that is necessary for holistic development.

DISCUSSION STARTERS

- When considering child development, why do you think the first two years are so critical?
- In what ways can adults ensure a baby gets the best start in life?

Figure 1.6 The developing brain loves to play. Lily relishes her carer's playful approach in the nursery

REFLECTION POINTS

- Every child is unique and will develop at their own rate.
- Child development is best thought about in terms of how areas of development interlink.
- It is important to recognise the variety of factors that may have a positive or negative impact on development.
- Observing children on a regular basis can inform a broader understanding of their overall development.
- Early intervention can be critical in order to best meet the needs of the child and their family.
- Inclusive practice is essential for every adult to adopt.
- It is vital to follow safeguarding procedures – this must be central to excellent early years practice.

Keeping the above broad areas of development in mind, we now turn to brain development, which is followed by Chapters 4–14. These contain detailed descriptions of development and "Brain & Body Sensory Development Pointers" (targeted descriptions of development at particular stages) alongside detailed brain growth, woven together with suggested activities. This content alongside film clips aims to keep the theory grounded.

Please note that if at any point you are concerned about a baby or child's health or development, do talk to a GP or health visitor, or speak to a nurse, doctor, or special educational needs coordinator at the child's school.

2 Brain growth

This chapter introduces:

- A cautious and sensible way to approach any new understanding of neuroscience
- An overview of the way the brain develops
- Research into brain growth
- Why early relationships matter to brain development
- The way in which the senses work
- Why the brain is attracted to new experiences
- A holistic understanding of brain parts
- The role of neurons and their work
- The emerging understanding of neuroplasticity
- Emotional well-being and its impact on the brain
- The notion of play histories and why they matter
- The role of emotion and memory
- The corrosive impact of sustained stress
- Creative well-being and its positive impact on brain development

NEUROSCIENCE ... IT IS STILL SO NEW

So much of the most exciting and relevant knowledge acquired from research in neuroscience that is relevant to the developing child and all that it has to offer in the realm of best play activities for children has so far either been applied too broadly or not applied at all. Although I lament this position, it is not difficult to understand why. This is, of course, a highly complex area and any attempt to simplify the knowledge runs the risk of being misunderstood. It is also an area which is rapidly evolving and needs to be updated regularly.

DOI: 10.4324/9781003309758-3

Figure 2.1 The developing brain loves to play. Baby Sunday's brain is on the lookout for new experiences to feed her curiosity in the world

The popular term neuromyth

In 2007, the Organisation for Economic Cooperation and Development (OECD) warned of the misinterpretation of brain science in educational settings – calling them "neuromyths." Torrijos-Muelas, González-Víllora, and Bodoque-Osma (2021) point out that researchers and practitioners need to be agile in their responses by utilising scientific findings as they emerge and suggest that closer engagement between schools and universities may well be the answer. The Pointers for *Digging Deeper* boxes are a nudge towards more in-depth studies for those interested in learning more about brain science.

Let's make a start on joining the dots

So, this chapter does not aim to achieve the impossible and overnight turn us all into neuro-scientists! Neither does this chapter intend to engage in all the debates around the latest brain research, but it does aim to provide a foundation from which students, practitioners, and parents can begin to value play for its blossoming potential to enhance child development as suggested by several educational researchers. For the sake of avoiding pitfalls, only generally agreed and established research is provided and explained in simple language for accessibility.

Three safety questions

A simple guide for the application of new brain knowledge might be:

- Does this make sense?
- Is it safe for the developing child?
- Does this new knowledge support best practice?

Figure 2.2 Stimulating the senses encourages brain growth

It is all about the senses

How the senses drive the fun for the *brain that loves to play* is the recurring feature of this book and remains the theme throughout this chapter. And, while there is so much that we *do* know about the brain, through fMRI scans for example, it must be emphasised that there is still so much that we do *not* know. Keeping that tension in mind as we explore play and brain development is the most grounded approach to take. There are several books and websites which provide useful information on the anatomy of the brain for those who wish to explore this area in a more comprehensive way. See helpful websites and references at the back of the book.

An overview of how the brain develops

The human brain is highly sophisticated as it controls all the body's functions. It is this very organ that allows a baby to engage their senses in a meaningful way. The human body's nervous system, which includes the brain, spinal cord, and a complex network of nerves, manages and coordinates the body's actions as well as the sensory information it receives. The brain is the primary component of this system. This nervous system has two parts: the peripheral nervous system and the central nervous system. The peripheral nervous system includes the majority of the nerves that run throughout the whole body and it carries messages to and from the central nervous system (the brain and spinal cord). The central nervous system maintains the body's internal processes, such as regulating body temperature and sleep cycle, and also performs the very act of interpreting sensory input from the world. In other words, it is through the senses that babies and children experience the world.

Neurons are messengers

The nervous system employs neurons to do the important work of sending and receiving messages to and from significant areas throughout the body. This sophisticated network constantly sends vital messages back and forth from the central nervous system. So, there are billions of neurons all bustling and working together to create a complex high-speed communication network. These connections make up the way children begin to learn, move, and feel. These busy neuron "workers" all have different job descriptions: sensory neurons send information from the eyes, ears, nose, tongue, and skin to the brain, whereas motor neurons do the work of carrying messages away from the central nervous system to the rest of the body to allow muscles to move.

Human interaction, the environment, and experiences

Babies are born highly dependent on others and their development is shaped in the context of human relationships and their immediate environment. Of course, the way that this unfolds is unique to each child. The genetic process mostly drives the development of the brain prenatally, although of course, it is sensitive to factors in the environment, such as chemicals and toxins. And, as Tierney and Nelson (2009:2) point out, "In contrast, much of brain development that occurs postnatally is experience-dependent and defined by gene-environment interactions."

An adult brain has about 86 billion neurons. Most of those neurons were formed before birth while the baby was in the womb (Goswami, 2015).

Figure 2.3 Loving eye-to-eye contact can build healthy relationships

Early relationships matter. When babies come into the world, it seems that there is a biological urge for them to seek out and establish human connection. Those who are in constant contact with the baby and child are immensely important in terms of how they respond to their everyday needs. The environment is also critical in the way in which children are encouraged to navigate their way around the physical world. Consideration needs to be given to how playful and rewarding that interaction with the environment might be. Responsive and sensitive interactions form and prepare human babies for adulthood. These interactions with a baby act rather like the foundations of a solid building. Researchers, such as Siegel and Bryson (2020), tell us that developmentally speaking, babies and children need warm and loving relationships without which they will invariably find it very hard to be empathetic, to make friends or to become an integrated member of the community. It matters how they are spoken to; how their needs are met; how they are responded to when they cry. So, it turns out that the more the baby succeeds in attracting attention and receiving all those warm positive behaviours from caregivers … the more she will try to repeat it (Davies, 1999). We know now that the young brain metaphorically "lights up" when a caregiver provides a child with what they need. Broadly speaking and in practical terms, this concerns the carer's ability to read gestures and interpret the baby's needs correctly and respond at just the right time and in the most sensitive way. The wealth of sensory experience which can be offered through play experiences in the early years is invaluable. Most importantly, the senses "feed" the nervous system – moment by moment. Moulding of the brain takes place as the baby and child absorb experiences from their immediate environment.

The social brain

Social and emotional development is critical to human development. It's tempting to think that formal education is the main driver when it comes to achievement in later life but that is simply not true. The defining factors are emotional and social competence: childhood must offer that supportive emotional structure to ensure the foundations are strong. Early experiences matter, childhood experiences matter, and every baby and child needs to know that *they* matter; they count; they have worth.

Human contact and especially face-to-face contact is essential for well-being. Children can struggle socially without the early experience of positive interactions with others. Every moment of interaction seems to count for the developing brain in the early years.

"We do not remember days, we remember moments" (Cesare Pavese, 1908–1950).

Attachment is key

The impact of satisfactory attachment and bonding from birth is an established theory (Bowlby, 1979) and the long-lasting effect in adulthood of a secure attachment in childhood is well documented (Adam & Gunnar, 2001). The young developing brain thrives on human contact. In fact,

Figure 2.4 Early relationships matter. Sienna receives the care and attention she needs at the nursery to meet her emotional and social development

in the earliest stages of childhood, the face could be considered the most attractive "plaything." Faces are responsive and they have an amazing capacity to change according to the baby's own expressions. Babies just love faces.

Ready and primed?

At birth, the primitive brain, which includes the brainstem, ensures that babies' systems concentrate on the most crucial aspects of regulating the body which are critical to survival (i.e., breathing and heart beating). This instinctive part of the brain also includes the limbic system and the amygdala, which is located within the cerebrum. The amygdala is well developed from birth. Later, the prefrontal cortex starts to help out in terms of how to prioritise information and make good decisions

Figure 2.5 Face-to-face interaction between mum and baby builds a relationship. Grace's mum knows that her baby thrives on eye-to-eye contact

about how to react appropriately. The higher cognitive functions, such as emotional regulation and inhibitory control, take much longer to develop, continuing right through adolescence (Sternberg & Powell, 1983). So, it is no surprise that children require ongoing, sensitive, co-regulated support from adults throughout this period.

How many senses are there?

The sensory system includes eight senses (three more than the five with which most of us are familiar: sight, hearing, taste, touch, and smell). The three that are less known are:

- Vestibular (broadly concerns movement and balance awareness)
- Proprioception (body awareness – in other words, knowing the body's parts in relation to each other and location in space)
- Interoception (internal awareness – the process which tells the brain what is going on inside the body)

Figure 2.6 Babies need sensitive support right from birth

Stimulating the human senses through simple age-appropriate play can promote mind and body development.

The sensory pathway and brain function

The brain receives information from the body's senses. The neural connections which are responsible for the perception of sight, sound, smell, taste, and touch are known as the sensory pathways. Gradually, the brain, according to usefulness, decides which sensory data to keep and which to filter out. Rich sensory play experiences can make a significant impact on the developing child's brain.

For the purposes of play and development and their *relationship to the senses*, the most significant areas to be aware of are described in this *very simplified* diagram.

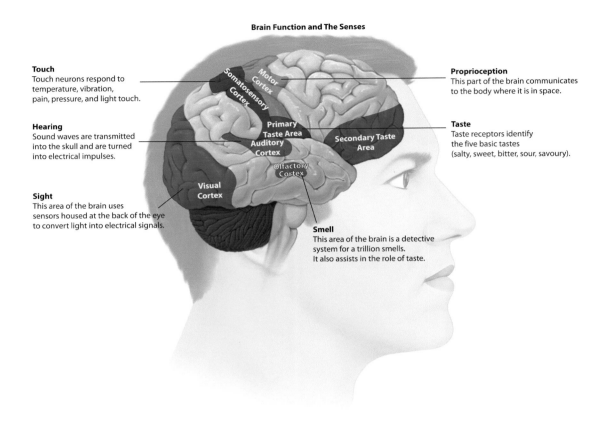

Brain Function and The Senses

Touch
Touch neurons respond to temperature, vibration, pain, pressure, and light touch.

Hearing
Sound waves are transmitted into the skull and are turned into electrical impulses.

Sight
This area of the brain uses sensors housed at the back of the eye to convert light into electrical signals.

Proprioception
This part of the brain communicates to the body where it is in space.

Taste
Taste receptors identify the five basic tastes (salty, sweet, bitter, sour, savoury).

Smell
This area of the brain is a detective system for a trillion smells. It also assists in the role of taste.

Motor Cortex
Somatosensory Cortex
Primary Taste Area
Auditory Cortex
Secondary Taste Area
Olfactory Cortex
Visual Cortex

Figure 2.7 Brain function and the senses

Brains love to see what is new

Play has one most fascinating function: it seems to delight in bringing together the developing areas of the brain and body. It has an astounding way of synthesising emotions, social capacities, and intellectual propensities. Brain scans reveal just how hard the brain works to make new connections; children's brains are constantly on the lookout for the "novel": what's new or different. The association areas of the cortex are key in processing "connection": this is where a fascinating phenomenon occurs. When children play and develop new ideas and concepts, it is through a process of chaos which occurs within the association cortex. It is as though ideas crash into each other, reformulate, and then appear. So, in effect, the brain goes through a reorganisation process to form a new connection. Of course, as mentioned earlier, this process is stimulated through coordinating new and novel information from the senses. So, it is no wonder that play and brain growth are happy companions along the journey of development (Hassinger-Das, Hirsh-Pasek, & Golinkoff, 2017).

The most important aspect of play, when it comes to brain growth, is the quality or appropriateness of the activity or experience offered. Neural pathways that are stimulated by age-appropriate sensory play activities provide just the right environment for the developing brain to flourish in the early years (Churches, Dommentt, & Devonshire, 2017). In other words, it is not the *number* of playthings or toys that a baby or child might have but their capacity to attract and stimulate the senses. Activities and experiences must not overstimulate and not under-stimulate the baby or child. It is a balance – in other words – not too much and not too little! And, of course, it is the quality of sensitive human interaction that does the best work for brain growth. I am convinced that if the brain could choose a plan for the day, it would make a list of gentle sensory-based play challenges accompanied by an interested and equally curious adult! Playtime is an exciting choice of nutrients for the brain. The brain enjoys a good workout – it likes to be challenged … but not stressed! The brain that loves to play is driven by a biological drive. There is mounting evidence that engaging in rich play opportunities as a young child may lead to greater ability later

Figure 2.8 Hana is thriving educationally as she is provided with sensitive ongoing support

on to navigate the ups and downs of life, progress through an ever-changing social, emotional landscape, and develop an appetite for new cognitive challenges (Vanderschuren & Trezza, 2014).

Fascinating brain facts

1 A newborn brain weighs between 350 and 400 grams
2 The brain accounts for 2% of the whole body mass
3 About 75% of the brain is made up of water
4 The brain uses 25% of the oxygen we breathe
5 Over one million new neural connections are formed every second during the first years of life
6 At around 22–24 weeks in utero, a baby responds to sound and at birth will recognise a familiar voice
7 The sense of touch is thought to be one of our first senses to develop – activated via neurons responding in the womb

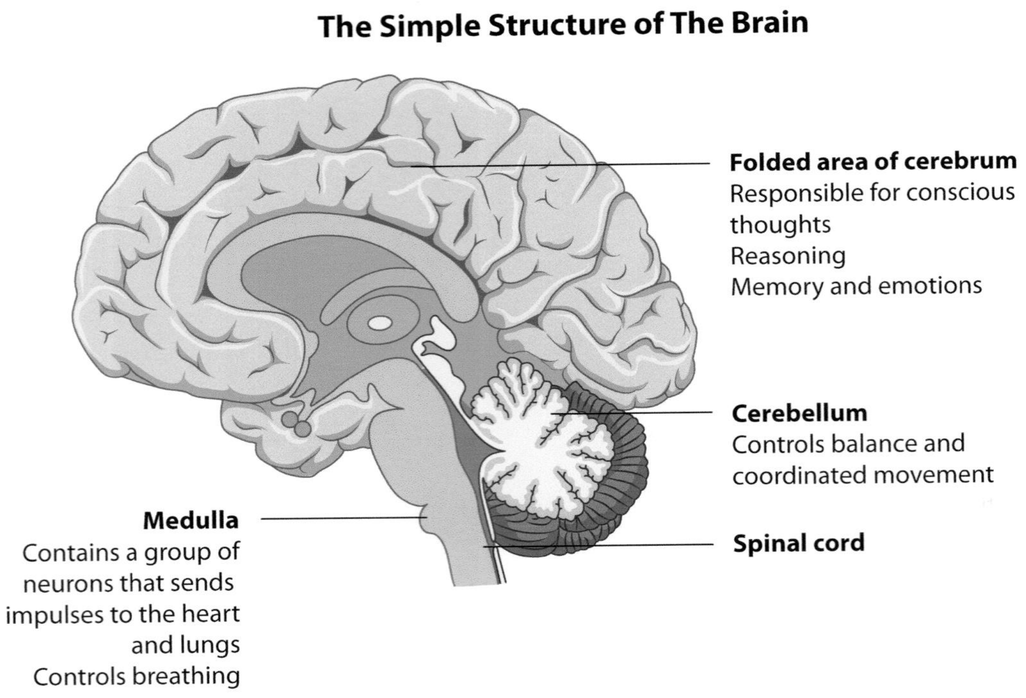

The Simple Structure of The Brain

Folded area of cerebrum
Responsible for conscious thoughts
Reasoning
Memory and emotions

Cerebellum
Controls balance and coordinated movement

Medulla
Contains a group of neurons that sends impulses to the heart and lungs
Controls breathing

Spinal cord

Figure 2.9 Simple diagram showing the structure of the brain

Integration: bringing the parts together

The brain has been subject to several analogies and descriptions, such as the "higher and lower brain." Siegel and Bryson (2012) explain the higher level cognitive thoughts as the "upstairs" brain and the "downstairs" brain being concerned with the innate body processes, such as fight or flight. They complete the analogy with the need to build a "staircase of the mind" which forms a link between the upstairs and the downstairs parts of the brain. Although these descriptions are all useful in some way, for me they are lacking in terms of a true sense of integration with the body, the senses, environment, social connection, and how this is impacted by play. However, these researchers do show a remarkable commitment to addressing this integration and offer many practical ways for parents to manage behaviour in sensitive ways. Numerous neuroscientists now implore us to think again about simplified mapping versions of the brain with solid regions for major functions of the brain (National Geographic, 2022). Now equipped with the knowledge that all these areas of the brain are constantly "chattering" away to each other, it is time to zoom out and think more holistically about the way it behaves.

Orchestral function

I offer the analogy of an orchestra, which attempts to ensure that the way in which the brain is integrated with other aspects of development is truly understood and that the role of play is factored in as an essential component in its smooth running. Of course, no analogy is perfect, but it does attempt to clarify the way in which the parts of the brain work together and how play impacts its foundations.

An orchestra consists of several different parts. These are called sections and coordination between the various parts of the orchestra is essential to overall success in functioning: the whole is greater than just the sum of the parts. In other words (for the sake of this analogy), the left and right side of the brain or the "upstairs or downstairs brain" (however, it is labelled) must work together and be considered in the light of the body, environment, and human connection. Again, for the sake of this analogy, imperfect as it may be, the conductor (the play experience) plays a crucial role in the smooth running of the orchestra. There are numerous musicians in an orchestra, all of whom have responsibility to listen to the others and are essential to the overall sound of the music. This analogy becomes even more poignant when inaccuracies about the way the brain functions are pointed out. Formally, the left brain was generally considered by some researchers to be concerned with logic, language, and a sense of order, while the right side of the brain was believed to be mostly concerned with creativity, and non-verbal thinking. However, this is now disputed (OECD, 2002). The brain is not as polarised as former researchers believed, as we now know that both sides of the brain work in a much more cohesive manner.

Therefore, if we see the conductor's role as providing the right environment for the orchestra and music to flourish, then acknowledgement needs to be given to each of the "sections." Without doubt, it is the conductor's ability to communicate to the sections of the orchestra that is paramount to overall success. Within this analogy, the activity (the conductor) needs to be appropriate and applicable at that particular time and stage of development. Rehearsals and guidance (suitable play activities and sensitive adult help with moving towards self-regulation) instil confidence for the actual performance (real life) so that the orchestra is confident and harmonious (ready for the world and its ups and downs).

Figure 2.10 The young brain and body thrives on human interaction

Lighting up the developing brain

During the earliest years, it is as if the developing brain is running at speed. With around 100 billion neurons at birth, the brain is ready for the firing up of chemical and electrical impulses. This causes pathways to form through the brain and central nervous system. Each thought and every action create a new connection in the brain. Then, if that is repeated regularly, a new pathway in the brain is formed, which then becomes the chosen route: neurons that fire together, wire together. This is a helpful way to picture the lighting up of the brain as it delights in getting exactly what it needs from human interaction. It is a phrase to which we will return again later. The "wiring" of the brain simply means how the connections are forged between one area and another. For example, when baby receives the response she needs when she cries, she can begin to make that essential connection between crying and having her needs met and … feeling secure. When she receives that positive reaction repeatedly, then a *positive* neural pathway is formed.

The fascinating role of neurons

Neurons communicate using both electrical and chemical signals, and through this process neural pathways are established. This is important to the baby and child's overall development because the networks of the brain influence how it processes sensory information, keeps a memory of it all, and the actual learning or cognition it promotes. Neurons form synapses with other neurons, and from birth to five years, this formation is at peak performance.

Importantly, efficient synaptic growth is subject to the quality of experiences the baby and young child receive and how carers respond to their needs. So, this popular phrase "neurons that fire together, wire together" is important when we examine the impact of the quality of playful experiences in the early years. The "firing up" of neurons causes connections between them. It turns out that high-quality interactive and engaging play experiences really *do* matter as they leave a lasting imprint or trace in the brain. Neuroscientists generally agree that the repetitive communication between neurons can create a strong connection between them and a network of cells emerges as a result. This "connection" could be to do with a particular skill, such as how to sort shapes into a box, or a specific movement, for example, kicking a ball, or perhaps a memory such as a park visited regularly.

The myelination process involved in the development of the brain and the importance of the sensory and motor areas

The myelin sheath is a membrane produced by two types of cells: Schwann cells and oligodendrocytes. Myelination is the process by which the axons of neurons are wrapped in a fatty covering, which helps them get on with the job of transmitting important electrical signals in a speedy fashion. The *timing* of myelination is important to consider in the early years as Tierney and Nelson (2009:4) point out: "Regions of the brain in certain sensory and motor areas are myelinated earlier in a process that is complete around the preschool period. In contrast, in regions which are involved in higher cognitive abilities, such as the prefrontal cortex, the process is not complete until adolescence or early adulthood."

Neuroplasticity

The term neuroplasticity refers to the brain's ability to absorb, form new interconnections, and make associations between one domain of knowledge and another. In other words, it is the brain's way of reorganizing neural pathways in response to new experiences. Norman Doidge's work in neuroplasticity (2007, 2015) was revolutionary and one of his most striking proposals is that the power of imagination turns genes on or off inside the nerve cells, which produce proteins that can subsequently change the very architecture of the brain. In essence, imagination is *speaking* to the brain in its language. In fact, neuroplasticity is the way in which the child's brain is enabled to make astounding progress in early childhood. We also know now that the brain is far more plastic and adaptable than we ever previously thought, and this applies even to older age. Although, without a doubt, the best time to nurture the process is during the early years, a period when neuroscientists agree that the young developing brain is particularly receptive.

Neuroplasticity and the impact of experience

Neuroscientists speak of experience-dependent neuroplasticity; in other words, the brain is an organ that seems to learn and change according to what happens in everyday life. With this revelation in mind, imaginative play experiences in early childhood are a rich "nutrient" for the developing brain in preparing the child for life's ups and downs.

Emotional well-being

Emotional "habits" are learned early on in life. The young child's actions are guided by their emotional states (Qin et al., 2012). In the simplest of terms, humans have a deep need to "feel" safe. Cortisol, popularly known as the "stress hormone," is released when stress levels are raised, particularly when safety is threatened. Stressful situations produce high activity in the right frontal brain (Davidson, 1992) generating a range of fearful and even socially withdrawn behaviours. Babies are born with a reliance on others to help them manage this kind of level of

Figure 2.11 Imaginative play "feeds" the developing brain. Hana is absorbed in her play in the nursery garden

stress. Their immature systems can easily be flooded with cortisol levels (which is exactly what they do *not* need). As time goes by, the child will start to manage challenging situations and emotions if they are confident that a caring adult is on hand to continue to help, support, and guide them.

Stress and feeling threatened

Several years ago, a lovely mum with a new baby told me about her older four-year-old son who was certainly unhappy about being usurped by the new arrival. The older sibling's behaviour was withdrawn and at times aggressive both to mum and the baby. Naturally, he acted defensively as he seemed to believe that his position within the family was threatened: the safety he had known previously appeared to him to be jeopardized. Mum began to take him out for regular spontaneous outdoor play which, she told me later, began to relieve the built-up tension he seemed to be experiencing. Creative play can help restore balance in the human body as it provides a soothing action for the nervous system. And, with loving support from mum and his aunt next door, his stress levels gradually reduced, and he was better able to regulate his emotional responses.

Daniel Goleman (1998) had much to contribute to discussions concerning emotional well-being and challenged the thinking of the time concerning the emphasis on academic achievement. He stressed the importance of the limbic system and the way it reacts to its environment. The limbic system processes stimulus in such a speedy manner that it can override more rational thinking. Quite simply, emotion and intellectual thought work in tandem. The lower brain, which houses the limbic system and other areas, is responsible for emotional regulation. But it doesn't end there, as this part of the brain has much to "say" to the higher brain with its executive functions. So, when the lower brain does not receive adequate "help" with any flooding of emotions, it becomes a challenge. The higher brain does not work so well when it is hampered by interference from the lower brain's poor messaging (Gerhardt, 2015). Suddenly, it all becomes clear when we realise that the higher brain (which is responsible for making decisions, planning, and making a "good call" or providing sound judgement) can be overruled by the lower brain. In contrast, when emotions are well regulated and supported, the limbic system does a great job in supporting these executive functions. Humans are not like robots as they need social connection and tend to function well when they are able to draw upon emotional support from those around them.

Learning to regulate emotions

For a child to begin to learn to handle and regulate their emotions, they need a great deal of modelling from those around them. Resisting urges depends on impulse control, which neuroscientists

Figure 2.12 Consistent attention to a child's emotional state can help with later regulation of their own emotions. Baby Grace's uncle is aware of his role in her life as she develops and he welcomes her into the world

call executive function skills. Self-regulation doesn't seem to come naturally – humans need those who are closest to them to help them on their journey, otherwise it seems at times that the messaging to the brain can get confused. So, early regulation depends on the way in which the parent or carer responds to those non-verbal cues sent out by the young child. In fact, it is important how the parent or carer responds to the child even during the earliest days, using non-verbal cues, such as soothing and cooing, gentle touch, and rocking to restore equilibrium. There is no doubt that even babies can be emotion detectives – watching for micro-expressions in those who are around them to work out others' emotions. It is well established that emotional regulation can be supported in very practical ways (Field, 1985; Fonagy, 2003). But what does this mean for play activities? Essentially, it is all about helping to form solid and secure emotional foundations so that a baby or a child has the emotional "space" and disposition which enables them to be alert and receptive to playful approaches by others (Jambor, 2000).

Play histories

As soon as the "social smile" emerges and the carer/parent and baby lock eyes, something astonishing occurs quite spontaneously: the right side of the brain in both baby and carer becomes attuned – in other words, activated and "in tune." This playful response lights up the brain. This is a secure base on which the rest of the child's "play history" can begin to be written. "Brain scans show that in the first two years of life, the mother principally communicates non-verbally with the right hemisphere to reach her infant's right hemisphere" (Doidge, 2007:226). Doidge continues by discussing how and when the main carer talks and responds soothingly, and through reassuring gestures to baby's everyday emotional experiences, such as having an uncomfortable tummy, it gives baby the opportunity to know what it *feels* like to get those full-on emotions under some control. It is role modelling at its very best. It lays down a pattern to follow and is the starting point to help baby self-regulate in the future.

Stuart Brown and Vaughan (2009), play pioneers, propose that how we weave our way through our own personal play experiences in childhood has a profound impact on adulthood. Play histories are fascinating. We all have them. The fact that they are playful does not diminish their importance. Through play in childhood, we have learnt how to respond to the world, the environment, and others; we have unknowingly prepared ourselves for our futures. For example, through imaginative play (acting out a particular work role) or learning some useful motor skills through practice with real or pretend objects, we establish foundations which may even influence our future career choices. So, it turns out that much depends on the experiences which were on offer in early childhood and how we reacted to them.

What happens if we miss out on these vital opportunities and there are gaping holes in our play history? It is well established now that with sensitive intervention, any deficits *can* be turned around. I recall a five-year-old child in my school who showed little interest in any of the activities in the classroom and yet seemed unusually alert to the needs of others around her. I was puzzled until I discovered that she had been a young carer for the last year for a very unwell mother and her younger siblings. She had certainly experienced no spare time to play. Immediately, I provided her with as much time as she liked to play in the classroom. Driven by her own interests, which in her case was role-play, she was able to work out some of the confusing issues around caring for her mum and siblings. From then on, her interest in playing with her peers blossomed. Later on, the more formal environment of the curriculum, such as learning phonics, began to be of greater interest to her.

Figure 2.13 Early playful and caring experiences have a lasting impact even into adulthood. Hana relishes the opportunity for playful interaction

Catherine Wood, an experienced SENCO, explains how play continues to be important at a later stage in schooling too. She reports:

When I was a SENCO at a challenging secondary school, it was clear that a number of children were not ready for the transition from primary. We set up a nurture group, with the intention of supporting their development and preparing them for the challenges of high school. They spent a lot of time as a group with one teacher and a teaching assistant. Age-appropriate play was an important part of the curriculum: board games to develop social skills; building bricks and craft to develop fine motor skills; and role-play to explore language, imagination and emotions. Over the year, their language skills, literacy and confidence grew and they learnt to trust the adults working with them and take risks in their learning. Some of them even learnt to enjoy school and the learning experience!

Play must not be underestimated for its contribution towards multiple areas of brain growth. Spontaneously chosen play in childhood appears to help develop the prefrontal cortex, which is the brain's executive control hub. This part of the brain is essential for regulating emotions, planning ahead, problem solving, and a host of other more formal operations, all essential not only for academic life but also for navigating our way more easily through life's later challenges in general.

Emotion and memory

"Early regulation is also about responding to the baby's feelings in a non-verbal way" (Gerhardt, 2015:39). This kind of "regulation" addresses a sympathetic understanding of the signals produced and how to respond in the most appropriate way. Emotion and memories go hand in hand and as such are key to understanding the importance of play and child development. Obviously, we all want children in our care to grow up with memories that are emotionally helpful.

Here is a very simplified version of the part of the brain involved in processing emotion.

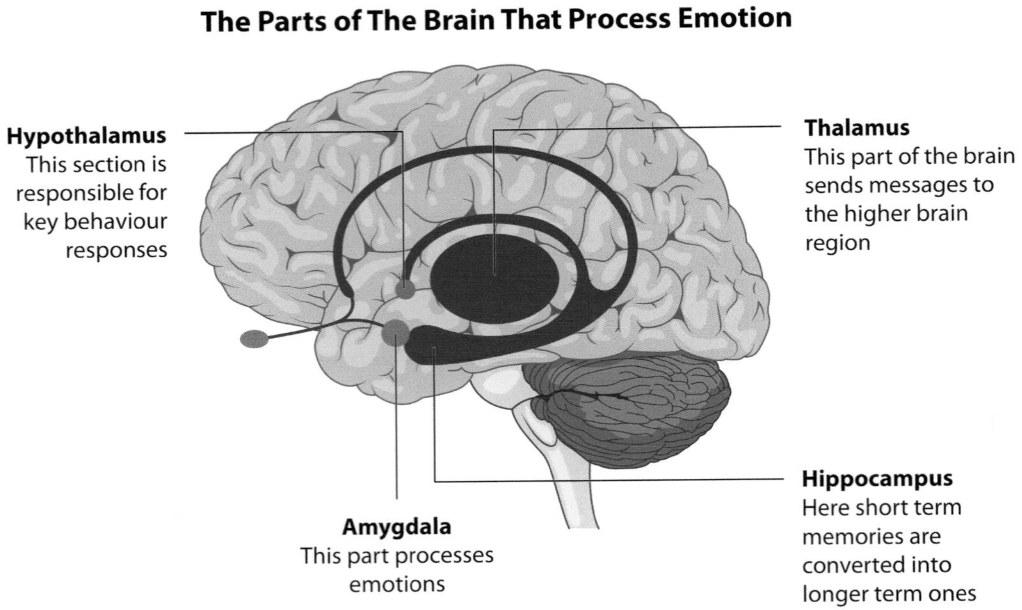

The Parts of The Brain That Process Emotion

Hypothalamus
This section is responsible for key behaviour responses

Thalamus
This part of the brain sends messages to the higher brain region

Amygdala
This part processes emotions

Hippocampus
Here short term memories are converted into longer term ones

Figure 2.14 Processing emotions

On the downside

Some researchers are concerned about what they see as the brain's rather puzzling propensity to latch on to or recall negative experiences. In fact, neuropsychologist Dr Rick Hanson (2013:27) proposes that negative experiences are so powerful that they seem to "shout" louder than positive ones. He discusses what is known as the "negativity bias." Hanson rather brilliantly describes this process in the brain as: "Velcro for the bad and Teflon for the good." Although not all researchers come to the same conclusions, this view of the brain's potential towards negativity raises important questions about how students, practitioners, and parents might ensure that children in the earliest years receive an adequate supply of positive playful experiences to override any possible negative bias of the brain. So, whether or not Hanson is correct, it seems that adults can do no harm in providing an abundance of memorable positive and life-affirming play activities.

Researchers believe that there is one area of the brain particularly active in this conundrum, which, as Hanson (ibid) points out, fast becomes sensitised to negative experiences. It is called the amygdala.

The amygdala

The brain possesses multiple neural systems which are on the lookout for core human needs: safety and connection. The system constantly questions itself: are these needs being met? And, considering this focus, the amygdala deserves special attention when we are thinking about play and emotions. This part of the brain is vital when a threat is sensed. Although it is only about the size of an almond, it performs a significant role in processing emotions at speed. It acts as an alarm call, urgently sending out stress hormones which cause the adrenals to release cortisol. This is a strong signal for the need to flee, fight, or even freeze. The amygdala has other purposes as well, but this is the function most frequently noted (other regions of the brain are also activated in response to stress). This is, of course, an unhelpful state for a child to experience on a regular basis. Importantly, if a history of trauma has been experienced then, simply put, the amygdala can trigger an extreme reaction.

Corrosive cortisol and the immune system

Toxic flooding of stress hormones (cortisol), particularly in babies, is well documented and has been a cause for concern for some years now (Gerhardt, 2015; Hosking & Walsh, 2005). Thankfully, sensitive human interaction offers a buffer against consistently stressful experiences and assists in the construction of a robust immune system and essential healthy development (Miller, Chen, & Parker, 2011). This "buffer" is a bit like wearing trainers with soft inserts to do exercise instead of suffering the impact and stress of wearing ordinary shoes. In much the same way, inflammatory responses impact the immune system. Psychoneuro-immunology (McEwen & Lasley, 2005)

Figure 2.15 Sensitive playful care and attention offers a buffer against stress. Nursery manager, Lourdes, is consistent in her approach to this strategy

has revolutionised our understanding of play; just "having fun" has a remarkable capacity to enhance health and well-being, tackling unwanted inflammation in the nervous system. Buffering a baby and young child against this potentially harmful state is paramount.

The good news about play, health, and well-being

The immune system has a memory. This discovery by researchers such as Goleman (1998) came to be known as the "body's brain" and was fundamental to an even deeper understanding of the relationship between early experiences and health and well-being. Loving touch releases the important hormone oxytocin, which protects babies from inflammation in their systems and has been acknowledged for its part in enhancing health (Miller, Chen, & Parker, 2011). The link

Biological Opposites – Creativity and Stress (Chaudhuri and Harding, 2008)

Creativity	Stress (or distress)
More alpha brainwaves	Less alpha brainwaves, greater beta waves
Greater heart rate variability	Less heart rate variability
Greater parasympathetic activity at peak	Greater sympathetic activity at peak
Greater relaxation, less muscle tension than norm	Less relaxation, greater muscle tension than norm
Greater skin perfusion	Less skin perfusion
Greater cognition and long-term memory	Greater access to short-term memory
Greater biological coherence (R/L brain hemisphere, HRV)	Less biological coherence (R/L brain hemisphere, HRV)
Better long-term memory access	Better short-term memory access
Greater fluency, flexibility, flow states, greater lateral thinking, enhanced problem solving	More rigidity in thoughts - beliefs values and paradigms become more inflexible, loss of ability to problem solving
Deeper breathing	Changes in breathing - shallower and higher, restricted

Figure 2.16 Biological opposites (Harding & Chaudhuri, 2008:79)

between co-regulation and self-regulation is now well established (Shanker, Hopkins, & Davidson, 2015). In simple terms, co-regulation means the way in which the baby is guided by a caring and supportive adult in the earliest stages, so they have a working model to draw upon for their own self-regulation in the future.

Creative play does its most brilliant and significant work at a molecular level. At a time when human brains are particularly "open" to new experiences, it could be said that play can do its best work. Play is an important antidote to stress as it increases levels of endorphins released by the brain, which are the feel-good hormones known for improving a sense of well-being (Harding & Chaudhuri, 2008). See the chart for a simple overview of the biological opposites of stress. Of course, this is very much just an overview – to explore this area further, see the "Digging Deeper" section.

The brain loves to play creatively

Vanderschuren (2010:332), who reviewed numerous studies of the brain's reaction to play, argues convincingly of the way in which the brain is prepared to make the very best of every play opportunity. "Together, these studies demonstrate that play is fun and that there are pathways in the brain that make it so."

Creativity and restoring balance

It could even be said that the brain relishes the opportunity to be creative. Creativity can be thought of as restoring balance in the human system. Creative play acts as a soothing action for the nervous system and seems to enable the brain to restore and rebalance itself – combatting stress and anxiety. The sympathetic system is generally acknowledged for its part in the commonly called "fight or flight" response; the parasympathetic system works to oppose and regulate it with the aim of helping the body to turn to a more restful and peaceful state. The system can get out of balance and needs to be coaxed back out of the sympathetic nervous system and back towards the safer and calmer parasympathetic nervous system (Harding & Chaudhuri, 2008).

Figure 2.17 The brain lights up at the chance of being creative and can calm the nervous system

Figure 2.18 Jacqueline. See video "Brain Development" via the QR code

In the next chapter, we look closer at play pedagogy as a strategy for encouraging a distinct link between play activities, brain growth, and general developmental progress, with the aim of demonstrating a fusion of play and learning. Theory and practice are intertwined; the videos discussed in the following chapters capture those moments when play and brain growth collide.

POINTERS FOR DIGGING DEEPER

The following references provide an in-depth reading in three areas:

Further reading for understanding more about the impact of affection on a baby's brain: Gerhardt, S. (2015). *Why Love Matters*. Oxfordshire: Routledge.

Further reading for understanding more about emotional well-being: Sapolsky, R. M. (2004). *Why Zebras Don't Get Ulcers*. New York: Times Books.

Further reading for understanding more about the biological impact of stress: Cicchetti, D. & Walker, E. (2001). Editorial: Stress and development: Biological and psychological consequences. *Development and Psychopathology, 13*(3), 413–418. https://doi.org/10.1017/S0954579401003017

DISCUSSION STARTERS

- Which creative activities could you suggest that you think might combat stress for a five-year-old who is about to move house?
- Is it true to say that "love is enough" when caring for a young baby?
- In what ways do you think that outdoor play could reduce stress for a four-year-old experiencing high levels of anxiety about starting school?

REFLECTION POINTS

- One of the most sensible and practical ways to approach an understanding of neuroscience is by asking vital questions:
  - Does this make sense?
  - Is it safe to the developing child?
  - Does this new knowledge support best practice?
- An overview of the way the brain develops is useful for understanding the importance of play.
- Recent research into brain growth provides even greater insights into why positive early relationships matter.
- The emerging understanding of neuroplasticity enables us to engage in a more positive view of brain development.
- Emotional well-being cannot be underestimated for its impact on the developing brain.
- The corrosive impact of sustained stress has a strong opponent in creative activities that boost self-esteem.

3 Understanding play pedagogy

This chapter will introduce you to:
- Theories of play
- The meaning of play pedagogy
- The purpose and benefits of play
- Play in the digital world
- Play and the senses
- Play and brain development

In this joyful film (mentioned in Figure 3.1, accessible via the QR code), you will watch Professor Victoria de Rijke and Dr Rebecca Sinker talk enthusiastically about how they have been inspired by the play theorist Professor Brian Sutton-Smith. They discuss the excitement of the book they are currently writing and the involvement of experts in a range of different areas of play, such as messy, risky, pretend, rule-governed, and "dangerous" play. They touch on the work of Professor Louk Vanderschuren: "How the Brain Makes Play Fun" (2010), which highlights how play motivates the brain to make connections. They also mention the important work of psychologist Donald Winnicott (1999) and finally refer to their own research around online games.

In this fascinating film clip (mentioned in Figure 3.2, accessible via the QR code), Naomi, a play therapist, speaks about her work and how play is an important "vehicle" for helping children developmentally.

Do take a look at the film clip (mentioned in Figure 3.3, accessible via the QR code), where Naomi now invites you to watch for evidence of "scaffolding" occurring in the films in later chapters, in accordance with Vygotsky's theory about the zone of proximal development, which helps us understand how to tune into children and support them just when they need it.

Now let's watch the film clip (mentioned in Figure 3.4, accessible via the QR code), where we can see 18-month-old Ethan playing alone yet starting to show interest in other children and their play. It helps bring to life how young children start to "connect" with others in their play.

DOI: 10.4324/9781003309758-4

Figure 3.1 Victoria and Rebecca. See video "Victoria and Rebecca" via the QR code

Figure 3.2 Naomi. See video "Play therapy" via the QR code

Figure 3.3 Naomi. See video "Naomi speaks about Vygotsky's theory" via the QR code

Figure 3.4 Ethan. See video "Ethan is beginning to take an interest in the play of others" via the QR code

Figure 3.5 Soon, children begin to play "alongside." Ethan is content to play "alongside" his brother at this stage of his development

In this chapter, play pedagogy will be explored alongside key theories and the various stages of play. This chapter will take you on a journey that helps to answer how play fits into all the other elements in a child's life and what is important for their development. This chapter does not intend to cover every aspect of play that has ever been researched (although the chart at the end seeks to offer a broader range in bullet point format for ease of reading).

At the core of this book is an emphasis on the integration of play, brain growth, and child development, so one of the key questions we will ask is: *what will this experience mean to the child*? This is very much in line with Ofsted's (2022) Guidance for Early Years Inspection Handbook for Ofsted-Registered Provision where an important question is posed: *what is it like for a child to attend the setting*? Chapters 4–14 will then make use of real-life play experiences offered alongside play theory. See *Play and pedagogy boxes* contained in these chapters.

DEFINITION

The literature on play is fragmented and no single definition of play has yet been agreed on, so this makes the whole area of play both exciting and open to new thought, but also difficult to pin down for ease of those trying to study it. Perhaps this is an indication of its distinct value to human development, so we need to grapple with it and see where it leads us for the sake of what is best for children and their developing brains and well-being today.

THE MOMENT-BY-MOMENT EXPERIENCE

I have spent many years researching child development by observing thousands of children at play and what has struck me most is how these play experiences unfold moment by moment before my eyes for each child. The journey of play seems to place the child in another mode of operation.

Figure 3.6 Imaginative play offers a fulfilling moment-by-moment satisfying experience. Lily and Sienna are immersed in their role-play

The child is then in a state of full concentration and absorption while situated within a bubble of timelessness, totally fulfilled and producing their very best efforts.

Interestingly, the psychologist Mihaly Csikszentmihalyi (1991) described these kinds of observations as *creative flow*, where eight types of experience can be observed. These "experiences" can be simply described and identified in play activities when:

- The child has a clear goal in play
- The child is empowered to act with confidence
- The act of "doing" and "awareness" converge
- Concentration is heightened to the exclusion of everything else going on around them
- The child shows a sense of being in control
- There is a lack of self-consciousness
- Time seems of no consequence
- The activity is simply worth doing just for its own sake

Certainly, Csikszentmihalyi's work brings to life the very essence of all that I have observed while children play.

CHILD DEVELOPMENT AND KEY PLAY THEORY

Professor Tina Bruce (2011), a respected academic, proposes that theories of play are particularly useful to adults who are interested in how children behave on a day-to-day basis. She encourages us all to closely observe children and try to make sense of what we see and how it might line up with what theorists are saying.

There are many ways the notion of play can be examined and explained due to the number of basic questions it raises. For example:

- How are areas of development connected to play theory?
- What are the stages of play?
- What are the benefits of play?
- What are the purposes of play?
- What is play pedagogy and how does it relate to the curriculum?
- What are the main play theories?
- How are the types of play described?

I will attempt to answer all these questions in a variety of ways, which are placed in context and embedded in each chapter for the chosen age range. This format ensures that a lived-experience approach is taken. For those wishing to understand more, the "Pointers for Digging Deeper" sections and further references signpost to more complex and relevant research.

AREAS OF DEVELOPMENT AND PLAY

Firstly, the purposes of play can be considered in terms of broad areas of development: social, cognitive, physical, and emotional. For simplicity's sake, only one or two theorists have been chosen to exemplify each area of development. The chart at the end of this chapter provides a more comprehensive selection of key theorists.

SOCIAL

Broadhead's (2009) research proposed that play is a significant way that children learn how to interact and navigate their way through the social world.

And, Parten (1932) developed six categories of social participation among young children. They include:

1 Unoccupied behaviour – the child is not engaged in play but is observing at times
2 Solitary independent play – the child is playing alone and independently
3 Onlooker behaviour – the child is not joining in with others in their play but watching others
4 Parallel play – the child is playing quite closely to others without real engagement but may imitate them
5 Associative play – the child is showing some interest in other children and may appear to be playing with them with some verbal interaction, but there is no real attempt to coordinate the play
6 Cooperative play – the child is taking an active role in play and starting to collaborate with others

COGNITIVE

Piaget's pioneering work (1936) proposed ideas about how children develop cognitively through their play. His main argument was that play is a way of building up mental representations of the world. He called these "schemas." Then, he proposed two processes for considering how children learn through schemas. In simple terms, these are:

1 Assimilation: integration of new sensory information into an existing schema
2 Accommodation: modifying the schema so that it better relates to a child's experiences of reality

Figure 3.7 Cooperative play with others can be fun as Sienna and Hana are beginning to discover

PHYSICAL

Hughes (2012) proposed that physical risks are developmentally essential and sought to reassure adults that children taking risks in play is the right way to experiment as it is critical to survival. Furthermore, Pellegrini and Smith (1998) lament any neglect of physical play and argue that it is essential to development.

EMOTIONAL

Erikson argued that through play, a child "relives the past and thus relives left-over affects" (Erikson, 1963:222). He expressed a particular respect for pretend play and for the way in which it

Figure 3.8 Children's emotional systems can calm down with the use of malleable materials to express emotions

offered children an opportunity to act out real-life experiences as part of their play (particularly any challenging emotions that they might have faced during that real-life experience). Erikson believed that play could help a child process confusing emotions so they could then begin to let go of any emotional overwhelm.

Now, let's watch this interesting film clip (mentioned in Figure 3.9, accessible via the QR code): the children have devised an exciting game of peek-a-boo, but when another child wishes to join in, the adult needs to help the children find a solution for themselves.

THE ROLE OF THE ADULT

There is much debate about how adults should behave when children are playing, and some researchers have quite fixed ideas about whether an adult should or should not intervene,

Figure 3.9 Lily plays a great game! See video "The role of the adult" via the QR code

Figure 3.10 The role of the adult in play is crucial to understand

whereas Pyle and Danniels (2017) point out that the role of the adult may vary according to many factors. They propose that it may be appropriate for practitioners in early years' education to be flexible and adopt different roles as they deem best for each child. Hadley (2002) proposes that the role of the adult in relation to children's play is the decision they make each time whether to be outside or inside the flow of the play scenario. The choice to stay outside the flow doesn't necessarily mean inaction – it could be a choice to use the time to observe and make mental or written notes to help them with future planning. If they choose to place themselves inside the flow, then they are likely to actively join in and participate in the flow.

One of the most delightful observations adults often make about children's play is their capacity to make believe, to suspend reality. Cremin, Burnard, and Craft (2006) discuss this behaviour as "possibility thinking." In other words, this occurs when children stop thinking about "what is" and start to shift their thinking to "what if." Of course, it is the very nature of play on offer that is pivotal and makes all the difference for the child in this kind of emerging cognitive ability.

RESPECTFUL PLAY APPROACH

Building consent into our everyday play time with children is vital – it sends a strong message of respect. As adults play with children and offer choices, it can help enhance their self-esteem. Reflecting on the language we choose to use also enables us to be constantly aware whether the play is adult-led or child-led. Encouraging children to be active co-participants in their play and learning through empathetic listening goes a long way in supporting children to feel truly listened to and heard.

THE ENVIRONMENT

Most researchers agree that one of the most important roles of the adult is to create stimulating environments for play and learning, but how an adult *perceives* their role while children are engaged in playing is highly significant. There are various views. Strong-Wilson and Ellis (2007) propose that the physical environment is itself a "key source of educational provocation and insight" (p. 40). Cadwell (2003) argues that through "provocations" (which are often resources) placed into the environment to spark the child's interest, the environment starts to feel "electric and alive" (p. 118).

The way in which an environment is set up is hotly debated. Vecchi (2010), discussing aesthetics, describes the Reggio Emilia approach as "a slim thread or aspiration to quality that makes us choose one word over another, the same for a colour or shade, a certain piece of music,

Figure 3.11 A range of books to explore can stimulate cognitive ability as Hana is discovering

a mathematical formula or the taste of a food" (p. 5). It can be argued that if children see that adults care for the environment, then it will impact the way they play and care for it too.

WHAT DOES PLAY PEDAGOGY MEAN?

How the place of play emerges within a learning environment will depend on the pedagogic approach adopted. It is rather like starting out on a journey and planning the route to a specified destination. The plans of the play provision will involve decisions about the amount of time and space which it is given, the resources chosen, and how the role of the adult is positioned. In essence, developing a play pedagogy will reveal what you think and value about learning and teaching, and then translate into what you do about it in your practice.

Play pedagogy is best thought about in terms of the lens through which a practitioner will view the purpose or value of play and how that really translates into everyday experiences for children. It is the starting point for action and planning. There are a number of different pedagogic approaches to consider including the knowledge-transmission model, constructivist pedagogies that prioritise collaboration and dialogue, and play-based pedagogies where children are believed to be engaged in learning in a natural way through playful experiences.

In 2021, the Government published its new guidance: Development matters – non-statuary guidance for the early years document (2021:10), which describes pedagogy in the early years as follows:

"Children are powerful learners. Every child can make progress in their learning, with the right help.

Effective pedagogy is a mix of different approaches. Children learn through play, by adults modelling, by observing each other, and through guided learning and direct teaching.

Practitioners carefully organise enabling environments for high-quality play. Sometimes, they make time and space available for children to invent their own play. Sometimes, they join in to sensitively support and extend children's learning.

Children in the early years also learn through group work when practitioners guide their learning.

Older children need more of this guided learning.

A well-planned learning environment, indoors and outside, is an important aspect of pedagogy."

Pedagogical approach	Description
Constructivist pedagogies	This approach concerns the way in which knowledge is transmitted by everyone concerned – all taking part and owning the process – often through discussion, building the knowledge together. The adult acts as a more "knowledgeable other" – embracing the Vygotskian theory of learning where learning is supported
Knowledge-transmission pedagogic model	This approach concerns the provision/transmission of new pieces of knowledge or insight from someone who is more experienced and knowledgeable, and the recipient is less experienced and knowledgeable. The vehicle for transmitting the knowledge is likely to be verbal or written
Play-based pedagogies	This approach concerns the role of the adult as one who is more of a facilitator in terms of providing an environment that may stimulate play experiences that promote children to be inquisitive and curious
Brain-based play pedagogy	Brain-based learning concerns the design of teaching methods based on scientific research about how the brain develops and absorbs information. A brain-based play pedagogy emphasises the integration of brain and body in its approach to the provision of play activities

The pedagogy of play demands some initial thought around two specific areas:

1 The purpose of play
2 The benefits of play

Once these two areas are explored, then the pedagogical underpinning for the adult begins to emerge as measured against the values and beliefs they hold.

THE PURPOSE: SIMPLY PLAY FOR PLAY'S SAKE

The works of Groos (1901); Isaacs (1932); Piaget (1936); Moyles (2010); Rideout, Vandewater, and Wartella (2003); and Pellegrini and Smith (1998), are sources of real value for the purposes of an overview that relates to play in the early years. In essence, play is frequently seen to be an activity engaged in for its own sake. In other words, children might play for the sake of playing: it often has its own focus, which evolves in the very *doing* of the activity. Bruner (1983) describes play as focusing attention on the *process* not the end.

Sutton-Smith (2001) suggests that play can be viewed as developmental growth and draws upon the disciplines of biology, education, and psychology. His claim that "the opposite of play is not work but depression" reveals just how high the stakes might be for brain development and learning.

THE BENEFITS OF PLAY TO LIFE AND SURVIVAL

Strong arguments for the benefits of play are proposed by several researchers in the field of animal behaviour, such as Tizard and Harvey (1977) and Groos (1901), who suggest that play "informs" the body and brain towards an increased likelihood of successful survival. Huizinga suggests that one of play's most important features is its ability to transport the mind away from the ordinariness of everyday life (Huizinga, 2014), while others, such as Karl Groos (1901), view play as the preparation for later life. Functional theories of play appear to assume that the effects of play are direct, mostly to do with preparation for adulthood, adaption, and survival.

Whether play is always a happy state has been much debated; however, it has been agreed that this is not a determining factor as children often use play to come to terms with things that are physically or emotionally unpleasant (Harding & Meldon-Smith, 1999). The seriousness of play finds greater agreement among play researchers (Piaget, 1951). Perhaps the most serious aspect of play is "deep play" in which the stakes are "irrationally high" (Geertz, 1973).

Figure 3.12 The purpose and benefits of play are very much debated

PLAY AND THE DIGITAL WORLD

One of the first most important pieces of work to emerge around digital play was in 2003, when the first large-scale study was conducted in the United States regarding the use of children's technologies by Rideout, Vandewater, and Wartella, which provided useful baseline data for future studies.

More recently, Ofcom's (2022) report looked at media use, attitudes, and understanding among children and young people aged 3–17 years. The top line figures for three- to four-year-olds showed that in the UK:

- 17% own their own phone
- To go online: 39% use a mobile phone and 78% use a tablet
- 89% use video-sharing platforms
- 32% use live-streaming sites

- 21% use social media
- 24% have their own social media profile
- 18% play games online
- 81% watch TV on any type of device other than a TV set

With a steady increase in the use of digital tools over the years, the issue of children playing in a digital world has become highly contentious. There are several notable researchers contributing to this important area of study, such as Marsh and Bishop's work (2010, 2013), whose studies show how through play children allow the digital and non-digital spaces to collide, for example by role-playing in real life what they have experienced in an online game. In other words, they transport that play experience from the online play environment into the role-play corner, seamlessly weaving their actions across the physical and digital environments. Marsh's (2010) studies found that children's digital and non-digital play exhibit many of the characteristics of types of play, such as rough and tumble play and socio-dramatic play. Sakr, Connelly, and Wild (2018) have also found some interesting and positive attributes of digital play.

Figure 3.13 Play in the digital world is widely debated

Their study showed the potential for creativity in the way that four- to five-year-olds used ready-made images as part of their digital artmaking. While other researchers view the digital play space as raising new challenges in a shifting landscape that is hard to pin down: Turkle (2012) points out that there is a potential for children to get "lost" in all the digital interactions taking place, and neuroscientist Susan Greenfield (2014) argues that digital environments are over-stimulating the brain, causing the young child to suffer from an overload of information and raising challenges in attention skills. Researchers, such as Whiting and Williams (2013), also highlight differences between online and offline social relationships and how physical comfort in times of distress can only be offered in the real world.

CO-VIEWING AND CO-CONSTRUCTING KNOWLEDGE

If we value the development of the senses in the earliest years, inevitably it raises questions around the capacity of digital media to meet those needs. In part, co-viewing or building knowledge together using media (co-constructing knowledge) along with the use of thoughtful follow-up activities, perhaps using role play or finding out more about a subject, offer some solutions. However, most researchers are in agreement that there is little to compete with the value of undivided human attention.

As we can see, digital play continues to be debated and remains a highly contentious area today with many researchers questioning if it can even be counted as real play. These debates also lead to several complex questions around whether it is an active or passive activity and importantly whether it does harm developmentally. The issues that are generally worth considering are the following:

- Is digital play replacing outdoor play?
- Does digital play offer children the same kind of social interaction as other forms of play?
- Is the sensory stimulation the same, better, or worse than other forms of play in terms of development?
- Is the fear of digital play driven by a greater fear of increased traffic on the roads and fear of strangers, thus preventing the freedom afforded to children over 50 years ago?
- Is the real issue much more to do with the quality or the time that children are exposed to digital media that is the greater challenge? Or both?

The works of other researchers in this interesting field are also briefly described in the "play theories" chart. Further discussions around media literacy and some of the advantages in terms of development in this important area are raised in the chapter "Play from around four years to five years plus," where the important work of Professor Christakis is discussed.

INCLUSIVITY IN PLAY

It is important to be aware that children begin to apply different frameworks to associate with male or female by around two years of age (Murnen et al., 2016). This has implications for play provision and the way in which adults speak about toys or activities can influence stereotypical behaviour. Creating an inclusive and equal play and learning environment will enable children to thrive. It goes without saying that all the activities suggested in the following chapters *must* take account of a child's unique stage of development and any needs they might have. Of course, freedom of choice and spontaneity in play is every child's right (within safe boundaries).

Having a clear idea of how to respond to any developmental challenge with ease and confidence is worth working on to ensure that every child feels valued and never excluded. Seeing a child progress is the delight of every adult who truly cares about the child.

Figure 3.14 Children can be spontaneous in the way they choose to move and dance in play. Ethan enjoys expressing himself through music

INCLUSIVE ENVIRONMENTS

Naomi, a play therapist, who we met in the film at the start of this chapter, says:

> I believe that play must be inclusive at all times ... it opens up endless opportunities and no child should ever miss out – regardless of disability or background. I've worked with many children who have benefitted so much from a truly inclusive play environment. As a play therapist, this looks like creating a playroom with a wide variety of toys and play equipment that is as open-ended as possible. In the playroom, children are given the freedom to play with anything they like, in any way they like (as long as everyone is safe). This means they are free from gender stereotypes and accompanying pressures and can express themselves in any way they choose. It also means respecting the emotional stage of the child and allowing time for regression and the learning and healing that can come through that process.

DELIGHTING THE BRAIN

As the very focus of this book is the close relationship between the senses, the brain, and development, this chapter must not close without reference to the value of activities that have the capacity to make a deep impact on the child. In addition to the suggestions below, each chapter addressing specific age ranges will provide further activities.

The benefits of sensory play activities are numerous; it encourages different brain processes while they explore the world. Activities that involve multiple senses tend to be more attractive than those that only employ one of the senses, such as watching television. If children are given opportunities to take part in sensory play on a regular basis, then the brain relishes the chance to refine this sensory information, which in turn improves overall intellectual development by creating stronger neural connections. The brain is learning how to sift sensory information; how to process it and respond to different stimuli. Here are just a few of the benefits of sensory play for children under five years of age:

1 Memory function is stretched through sensory play – sensory input is powerful and lasting
2 Sensory play builds brain networks
3 The soothing aspects of sensory play can be therapeutic – providing a safe space and even calming
4 Sensory play supports all-round development – language development, cognitive growth, fine motor skills, and problem-solving skills

Impairment	Potential characteristics	Potential challenges in relation to play	Practice foci
ADHD	Inattentiveness and/or hyperactivity and impulsivity	General delay in progress of play skills Shorter play episodes Failure to complete play activities Underdeveloped imaginative play Difficulty understanding or following rules Problems with social relationships Poor concentration Forgetfulness Low understanding of danger and risk	Outdoor activity can be particularly beneficial to expend energy Employ focusing techniques and wind-down time Use clear and simple boundaries Model and extend child's self-directed play Encourage turn-taking and social interaction Limit materials to avoid overstimulation Encourage the completion of short activities
ASD	Difficulties with social relationships, communication, and imagination Often but not always, intellectually impaired	Engagement in ritual repetitive behaviours Social isolation Preference towards routine and familiarity Low levels of pretend/imaginative play Anger or frustration Hyper- or hypo-sensorial sensitivity Difficulty understanding non-verbal cues, other people's point of view, risk and danger, jokes or humour	Develop clear and simple boundaries, reflect and track play activity Use alternative communication techniques Focus on relationship development Encourage ways of experiencing and understanding the self to encourage progress towards symbolism and pretence
Down's Syndrome	Distinct facial characteristics Delayed development in speech, fine and gross motor skills and cognition Poor muscle tone Susceptibility to heart defects, vision, and hearing problems	Slower play progress related to delay with gross and fine motor skills Repetition of familiar play activities Problems manipulating small play materials Lower attention span	Model and extend child's self-initiated play Encourage turn-taking and group work Develop social skills, confidence and independence Support physical play and understanding of the self Consider larger small world toys
Vision and hearing impairments	Fully or partially blind or deaf	More time needed to make sense of the environment, particularly for blind children Pretend play may develop more slowly and be less imaginative Preference may be towards solitary activity Relationships may be difficult to establish	Maximise use of available senses to learn about self and the environment Encourage turn-taking and interaction Support physical play to develop balance and coordination
Speech impairments	Difficulty producing speech sounds Stuttering Language delay Language disorder	Limited vocabulary and sentence construction Difficulty communicating with others Pretend play may be more slow to develop Prefer solitary play Relationships difficult to establish	Create a language-rich environment Play activities to expand vocabulary and language Model and extend simple play scripts Encourage turn-taking and group work

Figure 3.15 Characteristics of developmental challenges (Continued)

Impairment	Potential characteristics	Potential challenges in relation to play	Practice foci
Cerebral palsy	Stiffness, uncontrollable movements, poor coordination and balance, potential language and intellectual impairment Susceptibility to learned helplessness	Difficulties with mobility and accessing materials Early sensory and self-play underdeveloped Problems manipulating small play materials Low confidence in the self, own ability to make choices and to impact on the environment	Focus on confidence and esteem Support physical activities Encourage sensory experiences Consider larger small world toys Enable choice and activities to demonstrate cause and effect
Dyspraxia	Difficulty executing fine and gross physical movement Short-term memory problems Hyper- or hypo-sensorial sensitivity	Early sensory and self-play underdeveloped Problems manipulating small play materials Immature drawing skills and less imaginative play Underdeveloped pretend play scripts Difficulty following instructions	Support physical activities Encourage sensory experiences Model and extend simple play scripts Consider larger small world toys
Sensory integration disorders	Body has difficulty managing sensorial information. This could include difficulty in regulating information; filtering out what is not needed; discriminating information and/or the ability to plan movements. There may be muscle weakness and coordination problems	Avoidance of sensory activities due to confusion or feelings of overstimulation Underdeveloped symbolic or pretend play Repetitive simple play Difficulty manipulating play materials or coordinating the self in gross motor play	Support sensory play activity with particular emphasis on discrimination Avoid overuse of materials with multiple sensory outputs Encourage and support physical activities to improve balance and coordination Model and extend simple play scripts Maximise play opportunities that build on individual strengths to encourage a positive sense of self
Learning difficulties	No single profile, difficulty can affect one or many areas of learning, including: motor skills, language problems, maths/reading difficulties, and auditory/visual processing problems	Largely dependent on the type and extent of the difficulty May be a general delay in the development of play skills and also lower confidence and self-esteem	Ensure a full understanding of the nature of the difficulty Maximise play opportunities that build on individual strengths to encourage a positive sense of self

Figure 3.15 (*Continued*)

Impairment	Potential characteristics	Potential challenges in relation to play	Practice foci
Spina bifida	Muscle weakness Paralysis of lower body Curvature of the spine Bladder and bowel control problems Hydrocephalus Learning difficulties (all to varying degrees)	Difficulties with mobility and accessing materials Frequent hospitalisation or the need to deal with a shunt or catheterisation Delayed development of play skills Low confidence	Support physical activities to learn about self and environment Develop a positive sense of self and confidence in abilities Consider emotional support in relation to ongoing medical needs
Cystic fibrosis	Build up of secretions affecting lungs and digestive system Problems may include chest infections, coughs, stomach upsets and diarrhoea and poor weight gain	Frequent hospitalisation or need to attend daily physiotherapy or occupational therapy sessions Under-confident or lacking in esteem Potential delay in play skills as a result of the above	Encourage physical activities to support healthy lung functioning Develop a positive sense of self and confidence in abilities Consider emotional support in relation to ongoing medical needs

Figure 3.15 (*Continued*)

Conkbayir (2021:272) suggests that

parents and practitioners alike can support early brain development by stimulating each of the five senses during the daily routine. Giving eye contact during care routines not only helps to build trust but also facilitates young babies' developing eyesight as they learn to "track and focus with both eyes simultaneously".

PLANNING FOR SENSORY PLAY

A great place to start when thinking about planning for play activities that are rich in sensory experiences tends to fall into three areas. Here are some sentence starters in these three areas to help with planning:

Exploring:

- Finding out about …
- Investigating …
- Being willing to "have a go" at …

Active learning:

- Being involved in …
- Keep trying with …
- Moving towards …

Creating and thinking critically:

- Trying out own ideas with …
- Making links between …
- Choosing ways to …

The scene has already been set in previous chapters to persuade and convince you that the practice of seeing the world through the eyes, ears, and other senses of a young child compels us to place distinct value on playful experiences. But doesn't it all come naturally? Not exactly. All our senses, just like a muscle, need exercising and fine-tuning. It's rather like being introduced to a new form of music, perhaps jazz. At first it might sound chaotic, but with greater exposure, the nuances and intelligent chord progressions begin to make sense. Young children need to be introduced to a range of activities designed to stimulate each of the senses in an age-appropriate way.

Here is just a general introduction to the rationale for activities based on the development of each of the five best-known senses (although as stated earlier there are in fact eight senses).

HEARING

Attention to sounds takes time and practice. For example, there are high sounds and low sounds; there is tone, timbre, and pitch. Children need practice in listening and developing attention skills. A calm atmosphere gives young children the space to start to distinguish between sounds. Then, the next step in the process is attaching meaning to those sounds. Suitable activities can include singing, finger rhymes, listening to music, turn-taking in early conversation, and walks in nature to listen out for bird sounds. The use of home-made musical instruments to tap out simple beats that can be replicated is a particularly effective way of encouraging listening and turn-taking. It becomes a kind of conversation – I tap twice, and you tap twice. You tap three times, I tap three times – it is the root of a genuine conversation.

Figure 3.16 The developing brain seems to "soak up" the delights of music!

VISION

Right from birth, you will notice how babies are attracted to the light. You will see how they scan the near environment and at times try to fix their gaze. Instinctively, the baby will seek out the human face and make eye contact when feeding. Visual discrimination takes time and practice, so newborn babies possess rudimentary forms of most adult capacities. During the first six months of a baby's life, there is rapid development in vision, although full visual maturation takes several years. There are changes within the eye and the brain, and the connections between the two. It is important to know that baby's vision cannot develop until the brain is able to process this visual information from the environment. In essence, what happens is that the eye and brain learn to work together to process colours, shapes, and all visual information from the environment.

VISUAL DISCRIMINATION

When baby is in an alert state, sharing books with them is a great way to stimulate the development of sight. Board books that generally have bold black and white lines are suitable. However,

Figure 3.17 Babies love to look at faces

with the adult's understandable enthusiasm to share the visual world with babies, it must be noted that it is possible to overstimulate a newborn's sensitive visual system. Visual discrimination continues to develop throughout childhood and in the chapters to follow further activities will be suggested to suit age ranges.

TASTE AND SMELL

It is well known that the sense of smell is associated with memory – just one smell can evoke a long-lost memory. This occurs "because it has a straight pathway to the areas of our brain that

Figure 3.18 Smell and taste is a mind and body experience

handle emotion" (Ticktin, 2021:152). These two senses will alter and develop from birth and mature according to experience. Simply, just knowing that these senses take time to develop and need exposure to different tastes and smells (and that they will be developing preferences) is motivation itself to widen exposure in a safe and age-appropriate way.

TOUCH

The actual sensation of touch vibrates throughout the baby's body. It has a significant impact in the early years. It is well known that babies wish to explore everything and anything with their mouths and safety is a primary concern. Babies need a variety of objects that they can explore safely with their mouths.

Older children will benefit from the experience of a variety of materials both rough and smooth, hard and soft, for example, nature-based play that encourages touch and exploration.

Figure 3.19 Touch is often seen as fundamental to the drive to explore the world

Safety note: Please be aware that some babies and children are particularly sensitive or even allergic to some of the suggestions for sensory stimulation provided throughout this book.

OVERSTIMULATION

All babies and children need a good balance of sensory stimulation and quiet time, with some reaching sensory overload before others. It is important to be alert for changes in behaviour that are particular for each baby or child. It is also important to note that sensory sensitivities for children on the autism spectrum also vary considerably between *and* within individuals (Hazen et al., 2014).

CHECKPOINT CHART

Below is a useful chart to help you question reasons for providing a child with a particular sensory experience. Answering these questions can help supply the motivation to provide an experience that might make a significant developmental difference to an individual child.

Goal of play activity	Question
Empower	Is it likely to make the child feel confident and as independent as possible?
Engage	Will it cause the child to be motivated and inspired … and does it feel like fun?
Stimulate	Might it encourage the child to feel curious or to learn something exciting/stretch or stimulate their imagination?
Safe	Will it provide the child with the space to explore the experience within safe boundaries?
Life skills	Will it encourage a positive sense of self and family, community, and culture?

PLAY THEORIES CHART

This chart highlights just a few key points from a range of theories relating to play and how it might be beneficial to holistic development. It is arranged in alphabetical order (other play theories references are available throughout other chapters too):

Name and dates (century)	Outline of premise/theory
Chris Athey (1924–2011)	Developed the concept of schemas (a pattern of repeatable behaviour into which experiences are assimilated). Athey's theories have been influential in observations of children and planning for targeted early years activities
Virginia Axline (1911–1988)	Axline developed the notion of non-directive play therapy where children are believed to be able to heal themselves if they have suffered trauma. Axline chose free-flow play as a way for the healing to take place. She believed that "play is [the child's] natural medium for self-expression" (Axline, 1989:15). The role of the therapist is to enable the child to start the process of healing their innermost hurts through the journey of free-flow play

Name and dates (century)	Outline of premise/theory
Tina Bruce (20th–21st century)	Bruce (2011) developed thinking around 12 "play indicators" that can help practitioners be aware of when children are engaged in free-flow play. It is important to note that Bruce suggests that if seven of these indicators are present, then free-flow play will be evidenced. Here's just a summary: 1. Child is involved in first-hand experience 2. Children are maintaining control of their play by constructing their own rules 3. Children use their representations as play props when they play 4. Children choose to play on a voluntary basis 5. Children rehearse about life in their play 6. Children pretend in their play 7. Children sometimes play alone 8. Children can play in pairs or groups – this might be parallel, associative, or cooperative 9. Adults can join in the play, or start the play, but they must not take over the play 10. Children are wallowing in ideas, feelings, and relationships 11. Through play, children show their competencies 12. Play coordinates a child's learning and development
Jerome Bruner (1915–2016)	Bruner (1983) believed that children need to be physically active and to have first-hand experiences to develop ideas and the ability to think. He believed that play provides many opportunities for this to take place
Eager and Little (21st century)	Eager and Little (2014) argue that children will never learn how to take risks in a safe way if they are not exposed to any early in life
Eric H. Erikson (1902–1979)	Erikson (1963) developed Freud's theories about personality and the mind. He was interested in the link between imaginative play and emotions. His work also compared adults' play to that of children
Anna Freud (1895–1982)	Anna Freud was highly influential in play therapy work. She believed that play was a vehicle for supporting children to find their way through complex emotions
Friedrich Froebel (1782–1852)	Froebel started the kindergarten movement. His theories have remained at the heart of thinking about early years care and education. Froebel believed that children learn through creative play and that their learning is most effective when they are engaged in imaginative and pretend play, which involves them in deep thought. He saw great value in outdoor activities which encourage free movement and involve the child in exploring the environment. He also favoured creative activities such as arts and crafts, music, and books
Bob Hughes (21st century)	Hughes (2012:79–80) argues that play is fundamental to child development. He believes that children are gradually able to interpret the sensory experiences gained while at play
Susan Isaacs (1885–1948)	Susan Isaacs was influenced by the work of Froebel. She saw play as means for children to express their feelings. She also believed that more formal learning should wait until around the age of seven

(Continued)

Name and dates (century)	Outline of premise/theory
Maria Montessori (1870–1952)	Maria Montessori was a doctor who worked with children with learning disabilities. She concentrated on learning through structured rather than spontaneous play. Based on the idea that children are active learners, she developed a theory that they are more receptive to different types of learning at different stages in their early development
Mildred Parten (1902–1970)	Mildred Parten's work (1932) focussed on a child's interaction and described the *stages* of social interaction in play
Jean Piaget (1896–1980)	Piaget is regarded as one of the major theorists in child development. His pioneering work (1936) saw a strong link between *play* and intellectual development
Mary D. Sheridan (1899–1978)	Mary Sheridan (1977) was a senior community paediatrician and pioneer in the field of child development. She spent many years observing "real children in real situations." Her aim was to try to understand how children change as they grow older
Sara Smilansky (1922–2006)	Smilansky's play stages were intended to reflect a child's cognitive development: 1. Functional play (also called practice play) 2. Constructive play – children create or assemble a structure or object 3. Dramatic or symbolic play 4. Games with rules
Brian Sutton-Smith (1924–2015)	Sutton-Smith argued that the definition of play must apply to adults as well as children. His work attempted to discover the cultural significance of play in human life
Lev Vygotsky (1896–1934)	Vygotsky emphasised the importance of play during the early years as a time when the child acts in a more superior way. In other words, through play the child takes a leap beyond their usual level of behaviour or ability. The Zone of Proximal ZPD was defined by Vygotsky and Cole (1978) as a way of closing the gap between the child's actual developmental level when independent problem solving occurs and the potential to development offered via an adult/more capable peers' support Vygotsky was convinced by the importance of emotion: "Every function in the child's cultural development appears twice: first, on the social level, and later, on the individual level; first, between people (interpsychological) and then inside the child (intrapsychological). This applies equally to voluntary attention, to logical memory, and to the formation of concepts. All the higher functions originate as actual relationships between individuals" (1978:57)
Donald W. Winnicott (1896–1971)	Winnicott (1971) believed that play is essential to social and emotional development and that play and learning are very closely related. He particularly influenced our understanding of the important role of comforters (such as teddy bears) for children and called these transitional objects

Pointers for Digging Deeper

Over the last ten years, I have been questioning how parents might be better supported in managing their children's screen time (Harding, 2019, 2022). There is no doubt that most parents are constantly asking themselves if they are doing a good enough job and when the question of TV, iPad, or video game usage is added to their inner thoughts and struggles, then the doubts rise higher. When I looked at what research was saying about confidence in parenting more generally, then the evidence seemed to point to the need for encouragement and empowerment (certainly not judgement) and then offering a range of ideas for handling situations. As a consequence of my work in this area for many years, in 2018, I launched: https://www.tomorrowschildtv.com (TCTV) as a free online resource supported by Middlesex University. It addresses the digital needs of parents of children aged from birth to 18 years with interviews featuring parents, children, and experts.

In 2020, I was just about to complete a new piece of research (using TCTV films as a stimulus by way of offering parents a range of ideas that might best suit the age and stage of the development of their child). Then the pandemic hit, and this significant event, seemed to make the whole area even more important with the emphasis on screen time as a way for children to engage with learning. Previous research, such as Sanders and Mazzucchelli (2013), found that more general parenting support that sought to promote confidence was highly effective. In view of this, I was questioning if parenting advice around screen time should adopt a similar approach.

It turns out that the voluntary self-chosen strategies as a consequence of watching films on TCTV were effective with quite remarkable results demonstrating an increase in confidence and likelihood of taking suitable action out of the many choices that suited their family context. My conclusions were very much in agreement with the finds of others such as Ofcom (2018) and Livingstone, Blum-Ross, and Zhang (2018). There was little doubt that parents were grateful for a respectful approach to managing screen time in their home that took account of varying ways of parenting. Participants mentioned that strategies from films gave them confidence. Of course, more research is needed in this area – but the findings were hopeful.

https://www.tomorrowschildtv.com is a free resource to be used flexibly with both staff and parents.

Further reading reference: Sakr, M., (2019). *Digital Play in Early Childhood: What's the Problem?* London: Sage.

DISCUSSION STARTERS

The following questions can be used to help you discover your own play pedagogy:

- What do you think children really gain through play?
- What value do you place on the time given over to play?
- When do you think children should play?
- How do you think children should play?
- In what way do you think play can impact brain growth and overall child development?

REFLECTION POINTS

- There are many theories of play – all of which deserve consideration and can inform our understanding of how children learn through a variety of activities.
- Adults can choose a variety of ways in which to engage with children while they play and it is through sensitive observation of the needs of children in their care that best informs the way they behave.
- Play pedagogy concerns the values an adult might hold about learning and teaching which informs how they translate it into everyday experiences for children.
- The purpose of play has been described by many theories and researchers in the field far–all of which deserve attention and consideration.
- The benefits of play are numerous and mainly concern the way in which it can support a child's all-round development.
- Play in the digital world has its own complexities as technology is evolving at speed and research is constantly emerging.
- Sensory play is one of the delights of childhood – rich with developmental opportunities.
- Play and brain development are comfortable companions on the journey through childhood.

Over the next 12 chapters, play pedagogy and practice are demonstrated through further film clips underpinned by research and practical application. This is designed to demonstrate the integration of play, brain stimulation, and overall growth for real babies and children, seen through the genuine perspective of parents and practitioners.

The book Professor Victoria de Rijke and Dr Rebecca Sinker mention in their film is: *Challenging Contemporary Thinking on Play*, to be published by Springer, 2023. The research article they discuss towards the end of the film is: Victoria de Rijke, Mike Phillips & Rebecca Sinker, 'Playing in the dark with online games for girls' for CIEC *Contemporary Issues in Early Childhood* Special: Dark Play in Digital Playscapes. June 18 (2).

4 Play from birth to around one month

> **This chapter will introduce you to:**
> - The very early days of a baby's life
> - The theory of attachment
> - How a baby shows interest in her carer
> - Why the "environment" is important – right from birth

EARLY DAYS: JUST THREE DAYS OLD

Let's take a look at this short film clip (mentioned in Figure 4.1, accessible via the QR code), where you will be introduced to a three-day-old baby who has been born into a family of three children. We will meet mum and Levi (the older brother) again in later chapters with his younger brother Ethan. At the moment, the baby is feeding every half hour and they are about to move house, so life is busy! We see the baby sleeping. Then, when she wakes up, we see how she searches out the face of the adult taking the film clip and seeks out milk. Note the way that Levi responds to her in a calm and soothing manner.

Mum is alert to her baby's cues, so it becomes a conversation in a non-verbal way. Babies are born with a brain that is interested in social connection, but the baby's social understanding is dependent on how others treat them. This is a helpful way to picture the lighting up of the brain when it delights in getting exactly what it needs from human interaction. Do notice too the older brother's gentle and sensitive conversation with her – at this stage her name has not been chosen.

EARLY DAYS FOR ALI

Moving on to the film clip (mentioned in Figure 4.2, accessible via the QR code), do take time to watch baby Ali. He has been born into another busy household with older brothers and sisters. We can

DOI: 10.4324/9781003309758-5

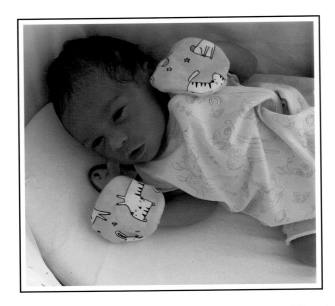

Figure 4.1 Early Days. See video "Early days: 3-day-old baby girl" via the QR code

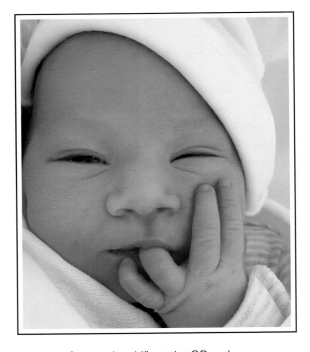

Figure 4.2 Ali. See video "Ali is a few weeks old" via the QR code

see in this clip how contented he is. He is a few weeks old and using his mouth to explore the world. A baby's mouth is the very first way that they experience their immediate environment. A baby is born with a sucking reflex – this is an inbuilt mechanism for ensuring that they will seek out feeding. Associated with this reflex is the tongue-thrust reflex – this is to support them as they latch on to a nipple and also to prevent themselves from choking.

EARLY DAYS FOR JANOS

Now, let's meet Janos in film clip (mentioned in Figure 4.3, accessible via the QR code), who is just a few weeks old. He lives in America with his Mum, Holly, who emigrated from England three years ago. Note how Mum is keen to stimulate his senses and knows that a book with black and white pictures is likely to attract him. Notice how he turns his head to scan the pages.

Figure 4.3 Janos and his dad. See video "Janos looks at the pictures in a book" via the QR code

Best practice: early interaction

The babies in the films are just a few weeks old and already keen to interact with the world. Babies communicate through emotions and right from birth, babies' emotional states are used as social signifiers (Shaffer & Kipp, 2010) to interact with others (crying, smiling, etc.). Adults need to be sensitive and respond to their needs; this way babies learn to trust their primary care givers. This helps them create secure attachment bonds which is very important for a healthy development. It is well established that the strength of first attachments can determine success in future social relationships. Secure attachments in young children lead to a template for more effective relationships later on in life. This "template" becomes an internal working model, which suggests that our early experiences give us a mental model of what we might expect from later relationships. When babies and young children see their carers as responsive to their needs, they develop a positive self-image, considering themselves as worthy of love and respect, and they are more likely to see others in the same way. This all contribute to healthy relationships with others later on in life (Bowlby, 1969, 1988).

BRAIN AND BODY SENSORY DEVELOPMENT POINTERS

Now we turn to examine child development more generally.

From birth to around one month

General brain growth

At birth, babies have all the neurons they will ever need but what they require is the right stimulation to help these neurons connect in the best way possible. Brain growth is stimulated by the sensory information that is provided through the immediate environment. When baby enters the world, she is equipped to use her senses to begin to make sense of the world. Babies use their bodies to communicate in the early stages and this involves all their senses for seeking out what they need to know about themselves, their environment, and the people around them (Roberts, 2002).

Hearing

From birth, a baby's hearing is usually quite well developed, and this is noticeable. They are easily startled and jump at sudden noises. In the womb, their hearing is well developed; they hear voices and react to noises and voices. Once born, research shows that babies have preferences for sounds they heard in the womb. Obviously, this means that sound sensory activities are important for memory. So, playing soothing music and singing are all good for sensory stimulation.

Smell

It is well established that newborn babies can recognise the smell of milk from their mothers. Developing a sense of smell is often overlooked but the benefits are significant.

Vision

During the baby's first month, she can focus about 20–30 cm away and she will seek out eye contact at arm's length and gaze at the human face. At around 4–5 weeks, baby will start to discriminate face features and prefer to look at the outside areas of the face first rather than the centre of the face. Her eyelids will close and open again to sudden visual stimulus and her head will turn towards any light. Blinking is in evidence from birth and is a reflex that will remain for life to protect and moisten the eyeball. Baby's eyes will start to scan the near environment, appearing to try to fix her gaze, and contrasting between light and dark.

Reflexes

At birth, the baby is already equipped with reflexes that are automatic responses to a stimulus, for example, touching her hand. A rooting reflex can be seen when her cheek is stroked. This reflex encourages her to seek a nipple with her mouth. The palmer grasp enables her to take hold of any item placed in the palm of her hand, and at about four months, this reflex fades. The "toe grasp" (plantar grasp) can be seen when she curls her toes if the sides of her foot are gently pressed. A term called "The Babinski Sign" occurs when her big toe curls and other toes fan out when the side of her foot is stroked – at around 12 months, this fades. The "stepping reflex" can be observed when, with the soles of her feet on a flat surface, she is held upright and then makes a stepping movement. This reflex fades by three or four months. Later, at around 8–12 months, it becomes a voluntary behaviour. The "Moro or startle reflex" can be seen when she is startled. She will throw her head backwards, her arms and legs will open (extend out) with fingers outstretched, and she will arch her back and then her arms and legs will close back in. Except for the sucking reflex, these examples of reflexes will start to fade within a few months – all to be replaced by more controlled movements.

General physical development

Baby can turn her head to one side when lying on her back and can lift her head very briefly from the prone position. She makes uncontrollable arm and leg movements. She lies with her head to one side while on her back – this is called the supine position. As her back is curved and her head lags because she cannot control her neck muscles, she requires essential support when being held. Her hands will be closed but she may open them when the back of her hand is stroked. She can bring her fist to her mouth and will suck rhythmically any objects placed in her mouth. This rhythmical sucking fades around six months (although babies, children, and adults can suck when they wish).

General social and emotional development

When baby is picked up when crying, she will usually calm down and may enjoy being cuddled. She will also start to scan the near environment and begin to show awareness of her surroundings.

General communication and language development

She will be startled by loud sounds and will generally quieten to soft rhythmic sounds. Baby will turn her head towards her carer's voice. Her varying cries all convey different needs, and she may cry quite energetically for her needs to be met. When she is soothed or content, she may grunt or make a squeaking sound. If given the opportunity, she will take it in turns to vocalise with her carer and may imitate expressions – such as poking out the tongue and smiling. To communicate her needs, she will try to establish eye contact and cry.

General cognitive and symbolic development

Baby will begin to show recognition of familiar faces and quieten when hearing familiar voices but is startled by loud sounds. She will gaze at patterns, particularly with contrasts like black on white, and shows great interest in faces.

PLAY AND PEDAGOGY

Attachment research

The films at the start of this chapter show how sensitive interaction with babies takes place through face-to-face *play*, which often involves talking to them, soft stroking, rocking, and singing.

All of these kinds of adult behaviours help develop the strong bonds of *attachment* which, in turn, encourage humans to thrive. The attachment theory was first proposed by Bowlby (1979). Attachment bonds are a defining feature of mammals. It is interesting to note that attachments in humans are characterised by bio-behavioural synchrony (Atzil, Hendler, & Feldman, 2014). It's fascinating to know that the parent shares an important brain network that is stimulated when they witness signals in their own children. This activity is supported by the oxytocin system which is the brain's way of encouraging attachment.

PLAY IT FORWARD

Practical play-based sensory activities

Name	Description	Age range	Resources	Activity length	Possible brain and body benefit	Safety notes
Hear my voice	Use a lively voice when talking to baby with variations in tone to help her tune in	Birth–1 month Also, suitable for baby in womb	None	A few seconds	Soothing and happy tones help to build secure attachment bonds with baby Lively sounds help to develop aural discrimination	Gentle sounds needed
Sing to me	During everyday routines, sing songs and rhymes	Birth–1 month Also, suitable for baby in womb	None	A few seconds to a minute	Soothing musical tones are attractive to a baby and can help build aural discrimination	Gentle sounds needed
Rock me	Cooing noises and rocking movements to help soothe baby	Birth–1 month	None	3–10 minutes	The combination of movement and soothing sounds is the start of a journey towards helping the baby self-regulate in the future	Gentle sounds needed
My first book	Share books with baby showing black and white patterns	Birth–1 month	Board book	Few seconds to a minute	High contrast pictures help baby develop visual discrimination	Not too close to baby's face
Hear me...	Rest baby close to your heartbeat	Birth–1 month	None	Few seconds to a minute	The sound of a carer's heartbeat is comforting and can help support the bonds of attachment	Under general constant supervision

POINTERS FOR DIGGING DEEPER

Bio-behavioural synchrony

The bio-social nature of synchrony appears to equip the infant in several developmental functions as proposed by Chappell and Sander (1979), such as homeostatic regulation and multisensory processing. Its place within the formation of a secure attachment to the carer is important (Ainsworth et al., 1978). The somatosensory data associated with close physical contact provided by the adult/carer result in a state of dyadic synchrony (Harrist & Waugh, 2002). Importantly, dyadic synchrony between infants and carers has multiple bio-psychosocial functions.

Research demonstrates that synchrony is a construct that provides children and carers with an interactional style that is significant for the child and adult. Literature (Atzil, Hendler, & Feldman, 2014; Feldman et al., 2011) reveals that central to bonding is the neurobiology of bi-parental rearing (which has been defined as bio-behavioural synchrony). The biological and behavioural responses are coordinated between parent and child.

DISCUSSION STARTERS

- Do you think that the parents and siblings in the films use the same interactional style with the babies?
- Try to describe exactly the way in which the babies respond to the attempts by the parents and siblings to communicate with each baby.

REFLECTION POINTS

- It is striking to see just how the babies in the films are attuning themselves to their carers.
- The theory of attachment helps us realise why playful and sensitive human interaction is vital.
- Early intervention is important because it can help improve the quality of a child's life.

5 Play from around one month to four months

This chapter will introduce you to:
- The power of the smile
- Turn-taking in communication
- Communication and interaction
- The "sensorimotor stage"

LET'S TALK!

Let's watch the film (mentioned in Figure 5.1, accessible via the QR code), where Janos, who is now three and a half months old, clearly enjoys spending time with his mum, Holly. She says that when he smiles, her world lights up. The film demonstrates how Janos soaks up all the attention that his mum can offer. He makes good eye contact and moves his head and body in pleasure as she interacts with him. You will notice how mum leaves space for Janos to respond when she chats to him. She also mirrors his sounds. It is the beginning of a genuine conversation and, of course, conversations are all about waiting and leaving space for the other person's reaction. In early childhood studies research, this is called "Serve and Return."

Best practice: early interactions

Janos's mum, Holly, spoke of her deep instinct to interact with her young baby even during the difficult days. Now she feels that she is reaping the rewards! There is no doubt that she was aware of how she was able to provide a safe and secure base for him. Holly said: "He's had a challenging start to life with a few illnesses which meant he needed to undergo several medical investigations and his reaction to me now is so rewarding."

DOI: 10.4324/9781003309758-6

Figure 5.1 Janos. See video "Janos with mum: let's talk!" via the QR code

There are also benefits of play for adults, not just children. Play can reduce stress and have a positive impact on parents' mental health state and well-being. Parents who are actively involved and engaged in play with their babies present opportunities for highly effective parenting and may feel less stress in their everyday life (Ginsburg, 2007; Sutton-Smith, 2008).

ALI IS PART OF THE FAMILY

Do watch the film clip (mentioned in Figure 5.2, accessible via the QR code), where we can see how Ali is quickly becoming a member of the family unit and is beginning to explore safe objects. He loves to see the world.

Figure 5.2 Ali. See video "Ali is a part of the family" via the QR code

BRAIN AND BODY SENSORY DEVELOPMENT POINTERS

Now we turn to examine child development more generally.

From around one month to around four months

General brain growth

A baby's brain grows fastest in the first 18 months of life. It doubles in weight in the first year of life. Baby will usually enjoy skin-to-skin contact which releases a hormone called oxytocin that promotes bonding.

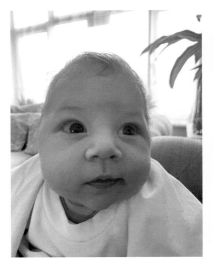
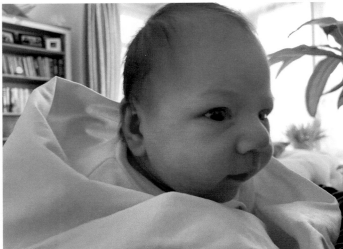
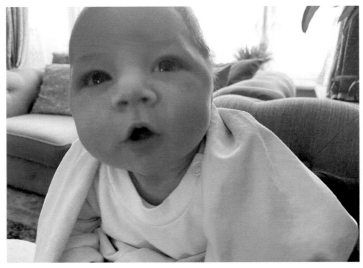

Figure 5.3 Baby Ali can now lift his head up and is demonstrating how he is gaining control of his neck muscles. He is keen to see the world around him

Vision

By around one month or two months, babies can focus their eyes on an object that is moving in front of them, such as a rattle. Babies begin to try reaching out for objects around three to four months, and this is an important development as their hand–eye coordination, eye motion, and vision link up. This provides an opportunity to introduce objects into sensory play.

Not long after this milestone, their perspectives change from seeing two-dimensional to three-dimensional objects and the benefits of sensory play with a variety of materials become vital. Early on, babies can see colour but cannot differentiate between similar tones, for example, red and orange are too similar. Around two to three months, baby will develop an awareness of where objects are in her environment and start to pay attention to them. Around two months, colour differences are more distinguishable for baby, and she can tell the difference between similar shades. Baby will prefer to gaze at high-contrast colours. By around four months, baby knows if an object is near or far from them – their *depth of vision* is now akin to an adult's.

Hearing

She will turn her head towards a sound such as scrunching paper. When lying on her tummy, she might scratch at a surface and notice its sight and sound.

General social and emotional development

Baby is acutely interested in social connection during her earliest years and is particularly alert to changes in playful facial expression. She will be starting to enjoy routines, which are beginning to become familiar, such as bath time. Her ability to start to smile tends to engage adults further and results in more smiles. Babies still fix their gaze on carers who feed them and are speaking around them, and show enjoyment when cuddled or when receiving affection.

General physical development

Baby will lie on her back, moving her arms and legs alternately or together. Her neck and head control are developing. When she is in a sitting position and supported, mostly she will be able to hold her head without a droop and her back is beginning to straighten. She will start to sit with careful support. When lying on her tummy, she will attempt to raise her head and chest, and extend her arms. At around three months, she is beginning to bring her hands together and can clasp and unclasp them, demonstrating how well her hand—eye coordination is developing (although at times she may still hit herself accidentally with a toy rattle!).

General communication and language development

Now, she is starting to coo and gurgle and can vary the tone and volume. When provided with attention, she will smile but will cry noisily for her needs to be met.

General cognitive and symbolic development

With alert eyes, she will focus on colourful mobiles and shiny objects.

PLAY AND PEDAGOGY

At this point, let's turn to thinking about how play theory can be the catalyst for enriching children's development.

The power of the smile

The film at the start of this chapter and several films over the next few chapters show the extraordinary power of the smile. There is a significant opportunity between the ages of birth and three years for adults to support the development of positive self-image (Goldschmeid & Jackson 1994; Roberts, 2002; Selleck & Griffin, 1996). It can be considered as unconditional care and attention – a powerful tool of communication to the baby or child that they can be safe in the knowledge that they are accepted. The micro-expressions of the human adult face are generally quick to be interpreted by the young infant. Body language speaks volumes. When a familiar adult frequently responds to the baby and child in affirming ways, such as smiling, this general feeling of being accepted is reinforced. Robert's work concerning the power of smiling at a baby shows that "… it is not simply a passive process; all the time the baby is learning by experience how to win the smiles … every experience is a learning experience" (Roberts 2002:5–6).

For the first few months of life, studies conducted by researchers, such as Gordon and Feldman (2008) and Landry (1986), suggest that the face is the child's most favourite focus.

All set and primed to connect

According to Piaget's theory of child development (1951), the child learns about the world through their senses. He called this the "sensorimotor stage" which begins at birth and lasts through to around the age of two years. Babies are all set to play through communication and interaction from birth; they can mimic facial and hand movements. This intuitive style of talking to babies, as discussed by Broesch and Bryant (2015), is described as "parentese," "motherese," "infant-directed speech," or "baby talk." "Social contingency" (the mother's responsiveness to the infant's signals) is a useful term introduced by Murray and Trevarthen (1986) which describes maternal emotional attunement in two-way exchanges. From two months of age, around when babies begin to engage in social smiling, they are particularly sensitive to these attuned exchanges, like a kind of silent messaging system.

PLAY IT FORWARD

Now, equipped with some useful play research, we can consider a variety of suitable experiences, some of which we have already witnessed in the films.

Practical play-based sensory activities

Name	Description	Age range	Resources	Activity length	Possible brain and body benefit	Safety notes
Mirroring sounds	Repeat back to baby her very own sounds and noises	1–4 months	None	Seconds	This simple activity begins to teach baby about their self-worth and stimulates aural development	Loud noises can frighten baby
Book time	Share high-contrast baby board books with her and talk about the pictures	1–4 months	Board book	Seconds	Activities such as these tend to be fascinating to baby both visually and aurally	Under general constant supervision
Smell the roses	Take baby out in nature and stop near sweet-smelling flowers and plants for a few minutes at a time – perhaps say ... Ah lovely smells	1–4 months	None	15–30 minutes	Such a simple and cost-effective activity does wonders for introducing a range of gentle smells	Under general constant supervision
Dance with me	Try dancing around gently to music while carrying baby	1–9 months	Any prerecorded gentle music	1–2 minutes	Rhythmical dancing has a great way of helping the brain connect sound to movement	Support baby's head

POINTERS FOR DIGGING DEEPER

Music is the language of love

Trehub, Unyk, and Trainor (1993) found that across different cultures, carers tend to use lullaby-type songs when responding to babies' needs for arousal or calming. Interestingly, they also coordinate their body movements to the beat. The connection that is formed between carer and infant is often described as having a musical dialogue: "The inborn responsive musicality of infants is a rich manifestation of the representation of purposes and emotions evoked by one individual's brain in the brain of another" (Trevarthen, 2008:17).

Colour preferences

Researchers such as Franklin et al. (2008) point out that for babies, any perceptual biases to certain colours may all be due to interaction with cultural factors that inform the child's colour preference.

DISCUSSION STARTERS

- Thinking back to the films of the babies, in your opinion which simple sensory-based play activities make the best use of their desire to communicate with those who are close to them?
- The role of fathers is important in a young baby's life. Read this interesting work around the role of fathers and consider how dads can be involved in the earliest weeks:

  Broesch, T. & Bryant, G. A. (2018). Fathers' infant-directed speech in a small-scale society. Child Development, 89(2), e29–e41.

REFLECTION POINTS

- The film clips of the babies demonstrate how vital social connection is to human survival.
- Young babies soon learn that there is power in the art of smiling!
- The start of essential turn-taking in communication can be witnessed early on in life.
- Communication and interaction between adults and baby is a sensitive and playful dance that reaps long-lasting benefits.

6 Play from around four months to six months

This chapter will introduce you to:
- How laughter and shared enjoyment lights up the brain!
- The meaning of "serve and return"
- How babies seek out social connection
- Why the brain enjoys human interaction
- Sensory-driven play in the earliest months

JANOS'S TUMMY MAKES HIM LAUGH!

Take a look at the film (mentioned in Figure 6.1, accessible via the QR code) where Janos, who we met in an earlier chapter, is now five months old and mum Holly enjoys making her baby laugh. This time she uses a song and actions to prompt joint laughter. Her repetition only serves to make him laugh more. At this point, he is still attending numerous hospital appointments and the shared joy of these moments seems to compensate for the anxiety she is currently experiencing. It is quite astonishing to realise that when the parent or carer and baby lock eyes, the right side of the brain in both baby and carer become "in tune": a playful response lighting up the brain!

Best practice: early interactions

The brain lights up when it finds "connection" with others in the world and smiles and laughter often support this process. Janos's mum, Holly, says, "Little one's tummies are particularly sensitive and frequently exploited by parents wanting to make their children laugh!"

DOI: 10.4324/9781003309758-7

Figure 6.1 Janos. See video "Janos's tummy makes him laugh!" via the QR code

JANOS CHATS TO HIS NEIGHBOUR!

Now, why not watch the film clip (mentioned in Figure 6.2, accessible via the QR code), where Janos is spending time with his neighbour who knows he has been in hospital and her winning conversation appears to halt his crying!

ALI EXPLORES THE WORLD

We met Ali when he was just a few weeks old. Why not take a look at the film clip (mentioned in Figure 6.3, accessible via the QR code), where we can see exactly what his mum means when she says he is much more aware of his family and enjoying using all of his senses to explore the world!

Figure 6.2 Janos. See video "Janos chats with his next-door neighbour!" via the QR code

BRAIN AND BODY SENSORY DEVELOPMENT POINTERS

Now we turn to examine child development more generally.

From around four to around six months

General brain growth

By around the fifth month of life, the sensory areas of the brain are building synapses very quickly. They are forming new connections easily. Neuroscientists call this neuroplasticity.

Figure 6.3 Ali and his sister. See video "Ali loves being with his family" via the QR code

Vision

Around four months, baby's eyes are working better together, and at about five months, her vision will allow her to spot even tiny things and, surprisingly, she may also be able to recognise an object after seeing only a part of it. Baby now begins to show a keen interest in toys and board books.

General social and emotional development

Baby reacts in interaction with others by smiling, looking, and moving. She is mostly friendly to strangers but can become upset when her main carer leaves. She is starting to deliberately seek attention.

General physical development

Around the age of four months, baby can start experimenting with ways to see the world better. When she is lying on her tummy, she may push up with her elbows to see more. Around 18–20 weeks, she will start to reach out for a toy rattle and shake it, and can bring an object to her mouth and away again but cannot yet release it on a voluntary basis. Around five and a half months, baby will explore her hands, and when lying on her back will lift her legs into a vertical position and grasp her feet. At six months, baby can usually feed herself using her fingers.

General communication and language development

By around six months, she is starting to laugh. She can exchange chuckles with a familiar person and enjoys social interaction.

General cognitive and symbolic development

When baby is in an alert state, she enjoys a change in her position, so she has different things to watch and take an interest in. Around 5–6 months, baby can now choose what she attends to – this ability to shift attention is due to refined cortical development. She will now show an increase of interest in playthings and follow colourful mobiles and shiny objects with alert eyes. Although a baby will begin to know that people continue to exist when they are out of sight, this seed of understanding will not yet apply to objects; if a toy falls away from the field of vision, for them it no longer exists.

PLAY AND PEDAGOGY

At this point, let's consider how play theory can be the catalyst for enriching children's development.

Serve and return

The films at the start of this chapter show the positive impact that an interested and caring adult can have on a young baby. "Serve and return" is a term used to describe back and forth exchanges between a baby and a carer. This exchange does not need to convey any specific meaning – it only needs to provide "gaps" in the conversation where baby can "have her say." It's rather like a game of ping pong and it's great fun for both the carer and the baby. "Serve and return" exchanges sculpt the very architecture of the brain in a positive way. Over time, these neural connections are strengthened and this all paves the way for understanding the nature of social interactions which are mutually enjoyable.

There is no doubt that babies who do not experience this kind of loving and nurturing "game" tend to fall behind with some aspects of language capacity. We now know that babies learn language through this kind of playful social interaction. Their experiences at home are crucial for building a good understanding of what being sociable really means (Tamis-LeMonda, Kuchirko, & Song, 2014). Babies who have experienced extreme deprivation of social contact are certainly at risk as they are not equipped to acquire normal language skills all on their own (Fromkin et al., 1974). The behaviours associated with attachment for a baby at four months are good predictors of how they will be able to regulate their emotions (affect regulation) and form attachments at a year old (Braungart-Rieker et al., 2001).

"Conversation" and turn-taking

Brown, Bekoff, and Myers (1998) view the very first steps taken towards play as the point where mother and infant gaze at each other. When the baby begins to smile (a social activity), it evokes a response in the parent/carer which in turn sets up a "conversation," whereby each contributes. For example, parents often coo and the baby smiles, and so on. Brazelton and Als (1979) view this sort of "conversation" as attunement. Feldman et al. (2011) found that mothers and infants synchronise their heart rhythms during social interactions. Importantly, it is the depth of the biological coupling which determines the degree of interactive synchrony between the infant and the mother. Recent research conducted by Atzil, Hendler, and Feldman (2014) demonstrated the coordination of physiology and behaviour between attachment partners. They also found that attachment bonds are formed through the processes of bio-behavioural synchrony. Their results suggested that parents coordinate their brain responses to the way in which their baby responds to them. This research highlights the differential associations of mothers' and fathers' brain activations with neuropeptides, which is known to be important for bonding and is correlated with oxytocin and vasopressin. However, research within the specific area of triangulation between adult, child, and toy/object is scarce, particularly in relation to bio-behavioural synchrony.

PLAY IT FORWARD

Now, equipped with some useful play research, we can consider a variety of suitable experiences (some of which we have already witnessed in the films).

Practical play-based sensory activities

Name	Description	Age range	Resources	Activity length	Possible brain and body benefit	Safety notes
My kind of music	Play lots of different types of music while you change her nappy	4–24 months	Choose upbeat music	3–5 minutes	Again, an activity like this can reduce the stress of nappy changing time (for both adult and baby!) and stimulates aural development	Under general constant supervision
Talk to me…	Take baby out in the local environment and tell her about what you see	4–12 months	None	5–20 minutes	Babies love the sound of a carer's voice – it builds aural skills and the beginning of understanding that the words we speak have meaning	Under general constant supervision
Read aloud	Use board books with pages that are textured in the early weeks and encourage her to touch the pages	4–6 months	A variety of high-contrast board books and those that feature faces and offer 'touch' opportunities	2–3 minutes	This activity attracts baby visually and aurally Touching the board book helps with the sense of touch	Under general constant supervision
Say my name	Use her name frequently as you pick her up	6–12 months	None	1–2 minutes	The foundations of language are being set through simple activities like this and saying her name helps build a sense of self-identity	Under general constant supervision

POINTERS FOR DIGGING DEEPER

Synchrony, attention, and mutual benefits to parent and child

A review of a wide range of literature regarding synchrony by Harrist and Waugh (2002) suggests that its form changes and moulds according to the age and stage of the child (and other factors). There are benefits to all-round development to the child and positive changes in the parents' brains (Feldman et al., 2011; Tronick & Gianino, 1986), and this is defined as synchrony (the matching of emotional state). However, it should be noted that such synchronistic interactions are typically characterised by the way in which a parent approaches their child. The notion of synchrony includes a focus on mutual responsiveness, termed "reciprocal responsiveness" (Ainsworth, Bell, & Stayton, 1974). This state has also been described in other terms by researchers, such as "affect attunement" (Stern et al., 1985) and "dyadic affect regulation" (Hann et al., 1994).

DISCUSSION STARTERS

- Consider the shared laughter in the film with Janos, and with fun in mind, name two games that a carer and baby can play together that could stimulate further "turn taking" between them.
- Read about the work of the researchers cited below. How might it apply to the "Serve and return" exchanges seen in the film?

De Luna, J. E. & Wang, D. C. (2021). Child traumatic stress and the sacred: Neurobiologically informed interventions for therapists and parents. *Religions*, *12*, 163. https://doi.org/10.3390/rel12030163

REFLECTION POINTS

- The babies in the films demonstrate the importance of human interaction at such an early age and "shared enjoyment."
- There is substantial evidence to show that babies enjoy building their communication skills.
- The brain enjoys finding "connection" with others in the world and builds essential neural pathways.
- Research in the area of "serve and return" demonstrates the joy of early communication and why "turn taking" is an important skill to develop.

7 Play from around six months to nine months

This chapter will introduce you to:
- The face as a source of play
- The brain and mutual engagement
- The fascinating introduction of taste
- Music and the developing brain
- Mutual engagement
- Stimulation of the senses through playing

JANOS EXPLORES FACES

Janos is now six months old (we have met him earlier) – why not watch the film (mentioned in Figure 7.1, accessible via the QR code), where you will witness a preference for exploring faces – even if they are on the front of a box! The human face is truly fascinating.

JANOS EXPLORES FOOD: SENSORY EXPERIENCES

In this film clip (mentioned in Figure 7.2, accessible via the QR code), we can observe Janos tasting solid food for the first time at six months old. As his taste buds are activated, we see the impact on his face as his whole body reacts to the new sensation.

JANOS EXPLORES LANGUAGE

Take a look at the film clip (mentioned in Figure 7.3, accessible via the QR code), where Janos, who is now nine months old, is enjoying rhymes. You will see just how the types of stimuli infants and children are exposed to can positively help shape both the brain and behaviour.

DOI: 10.4324/9781003309758-8

Figure 7.1 Janos. See video "Janos explores faces" via the QR code

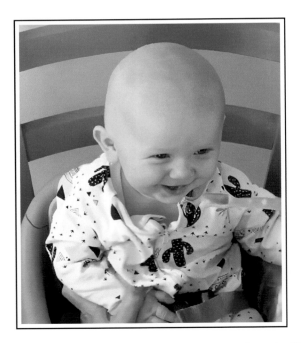

Figure 7.2 Janos. See video "Janos thinks … that tastes interesting!" via the QR code

Figure 7.3 Janos. See video "Janos enjoying rhymes" via the QR code

Best practice: early interactions

Holly, Janos's mum is fascinated by her young son's desire to connect with her and she exploits every opportunity to encourage him to make eye contact with her. She is aware of the need to give encouraging feedback in terms of smiles and laughter to make the most of every moment.

THE BRAIN ENJOYS SOCIAL INTERACTION

Why not watch me in this short film clip (mentioned in Figure 7.4, accessible via the QR code) where I share with you the research I undertook for Fisher Price. The results show that shared interest, close proximity, and social connection really *are* what the brain is interested in at this stage.

BRAIN AND BODY SENSORY DEVELOPMENT POINTERS

Now we turn to examine child development more generally.

Figure 7.4 Jacqueline. See video "The author speaks about her research" via the QR code

Around six to nine months

General brain growth

Between 6 and 12 months, the prefrontal cortex is very busy. It experiences a burst in synaptic connections. Of course, this is all dependent on what baby experiences from those around them. Playful interaction is essential alongside having their needs met.

Vision

By around eight months, baby's vision is quite well developed. She can see longer distances and she can recognise people and objects across a small room. Information is being processed binocularly and her vision is very sharp. She may even want to point at toys or objects she sees … and wants!

Hearing

She turns to hear her carer's voice – even when they are a little distance away.

General social and emotional development

Baby will begin to recognise familiar faces and is now likely to begin to show a friendly interest in unfamiliar people but with some shyness. She may continue to be a little upset if the main carer leaves the room. Around this time (and sometimes earlier), she will start to show an interest in finger games. Baby may be calmed when upset if held, rocked, spoken to, or sung to with a soothing voice. She will deliberately start to seek out attention and become more aware of others' emotions. She explores objects with both hands and may offer favoured objects to others.

General physical development

Around this age, baby can now place more weight on her legs if held and supported. At six months, she can use her whole hand to hold or take a toy/object using a typical two-handed approach. This is called a palmar grasp. From around six months onwards, baby will grasp a toy and pass it from one hand to the other. Around six months, she begins to sit with support and by nine months she will tend to sit well without support. She likes to adjust her position to see something of interest.

General communication and language development

Baby now begins to explore and enjoy sounds in the environment and will laugh wholeheartedly. She is likely to enjoy shaking a rattle to make a noise. She might imitate familiar sounds and use melodic tones. She will begin to show an understanding of words that are used frequently. Around this stage, she will start to show comprehension of the meaning of some words or phrases by her actions, for example, she might wave bye-bye. She will also begin to understand the meaning of familiar words, such as "mama" and "dada," "up" and "down." At around six months, baby will start using sounds that express emotion and may start to copy sounds she hears, such as "ma," and "da."

General cognitive and symbolic development

Around this age, baby begins to show an even greater interest in books and her eyes will scan the pictures on the pages. Baby is likely to watch what familiar adults are doing. She is starting to understand cause and effect; for example, if something is thrown down, it will make a sound.

PLAY AND PEDAGOGY

Drawing again on the films showing the interaction between adults and baby, let's turn now to consider how play theory can underpin understanding.

Mutual engagement

Trevarthen's (2008) work is important because it discusses how babies learn through the senses and the way in which playful interactions build meaningful relationships. He discussed the capacity right from birth for mutual engagement and times of "harmony" between adult and baby. At around the age of 9–12 months, their attention shifts to include objects. In other words, infants are capable of sharing attention by focussing on an external object, such as a toy with a parent/carer.

Let's sing!

Research by Franco, Suttora, Spinelli, Kozar, and Fasolo (2021) concerning the importance of singing in the early months revealed promising results. Parents who engaged in frequent singing to their babies at six months had a positive impact on their babies' language development in the second year. These results were replicated by Papadimitriou et al. (2021). Furthermore, experimental research has shown that infant discrimination of speech sounds (a very important aspect in language acquisition) is facilitated in singing contexts (Falk et al., 2021). Importantly, this work demonstrated that an increase in early musical interactions may possibly counteract any linguistic disadvantages in a variety of contexts later on.

PLAY IT FORWARD

Building on the useful play research examined above, we can consider a variety of suitable experiences (some of which we have already witnessed in the films).

Practical play-based sensory activities

Name	Description	Age range	Resources	Activity length	Possible brain and body benefit	Safety notes
Take action	Try action rhymes – learn short, engaging, repetitive finger rhymes, such as "Round and round the garden"	4/5–9 months	None	2–3 minutes	At this age, babies do not understand the words yet, but the visual cues provided by simple activities like this go a long way to helping that process. The adult's hands moving in such a way will be engaging and will prepare them for joining in with such activities when they are developmentally ready. The eye contact that the adult makes with the baby together with exaggerated facial expressions are enthralling to baby. These are important non-verbal cues	Under general constant supervision
Sing out…	Sing as you go about doing particular routines and have distinct tunes for each one	6–12 months	None	2–3 minutes	Helps develop attention and interaction skills so baby can learn to anticipate an event and develop her understanding of routines	Under general constant supervision
Clapping	Capture attention by gentle clapping and smiling at the same time	5/6–12 months	None	Seconds	This activity gently attracts baby visually and aurally	Loud noises can frighten baby
Bouncy bounce	Even a young baby can enjoy the movement of a ball – tracking it with their eyes, and as they mature, they can enjoy activities such as having the ball rolled to them and attempting to return it	6 months to 5 years	Balls with different textures	1–2 minutes	Balls offer babies and young children the opportunity to develop hand–eye coordination and general motor control	Under general constant supervision

POINTERS FOR DIGGING DEEPER

Here is an opportunity to dig deeper by watching the film (mentioned in Figure 7.5, accessible via the QR code) where Dr Fabia Franco describes her fascinating research into the kind of musical activities parents and carers provide at home and how it supports early language development for infants. Then, she discusses the correlation between musical activities and language development.

Interpersonal neurobiology

Louis Cozolino (2014), in his book: *The Neuroscience of Human Relationships*, discusses the parent and infant relationship and claims that the brains of both mother and baby are shaped by their joint interaction. Cozolino expresses this process as interpersonal neurobiology (the way in which genes and environments interact and impact each other through that very relationship). It is described as a reactive neuroplastic process which can make changes in the biochemistry of the brain, altering its very structures. Importantly, there is mounting evidence in the neurobiology of early childhood development, that young children develop through their relationships with the

Figure 7.5 Dr Fabia Franco. See video "Musical hits!" via the QR code

most significant people in their lives (Bronfenbrenner, 1988; Gerhardt, 2015). The importance of this process is evident across all cultures irrespective of child-rearing practices (World Health Organization, 2004).

Dyadic characteristics

During the baby's second six months of life, both baby and adult begin to match the cues/signals supplied by the other. Synchrony is viewed as a dyadic characteristic. This more than adequately describes the interaction between a child and a parent and is an observable dyadic interaction. Interestingly, this dyadic characteristic is mutually regulated and reciprocal in nature. In other words, the action is reflected or mirrored back to the person giving it.

Joint attention

One study in "joint attention" of an object between a child and carer, after the child's first six months of life, was conducted by Moore and Dunham (1995). This interesting and unique study concludes that joint visual attention is possible and vital for social development. It also proposes that infants have an evolving awareness of how attention can be shared with a parent/carer and object. Joint attentional focus (as described by Tomasello & Farrar, 1986) demonstrates that when the parent and the child are focussing on a shared object/toy, the child directs the behaviour of the parent in an overt manner. There is, however, much continuing debate around the interpretation of the results. Tsuk (1998) found that within mutuality and reciprocity, parents and children exhibit the same state of enthusiasm. An empirical study undertaken by Lay, Waters, and Park (1989) suggests that toddler–carer synchrony, perhaps engaged in object play, such as bricks, increases enjoyment for the child.

DISCUSSION STARTERS

- Watch a selection of previously viewed film clips in this book and consider how the adults build fun into each experience. What do you think humour offers the baby?
- Can you recall a time when you have observed a carer and a young child engage in an activity (toy or game) that genuinely appeared to enthral them both? If so, what benefits do you think both parties derived from the experience?
- In what ways can stereotypical play be avoided in the earliest months?
- What potential negative messages could stereotypical play convey to the developing brain?

REFLECTION POINTS

- The film clips of Janos show how the brain relishes mutual engagement.
- The attraction of the human face intrigues the young baby.
- Research is demonstrating that songs and rhymes have a truly amazing and lasting impact on the child particularly in the area of language development.
- When adults engage in play with babies with "shared interest" and in close proximity, the brain delights in the meaningful social connection that is offered.
- Play and learning through the senses is a delightful stimulus for the developing brain.

8 Play from around nine months to 12 months

This chapter will introduce you to:
- The value of playful sensory stimulation for this age range
- "Provocations" and the joy of new play experiences
- The notion of how imitation impacts development
- The value of first-hand experience
- Play and the soothing effect of comforters
- The meaning of object permanence

JANOS EXPLORES NEW SIGHTS, SOUNDS, AND SMELLS

Why not take a look at this delightful film clip (mentioned in Figure 8.1, accessible via the QR code) where Janos, who we have met in earlier chapters, is now 11 months old and is experiencing the sea for the first time. This clip enables us as viewers to almost *live this experience* with Janos through witnessing his body movements. We can observe a variety of expressions on his face as he encounters the smell of the sea, the sound of the waves, and the sight of the waves for the first time. He immerses himself in this new first-hand sensory experience. With mum close by, he is confident to fully enter into the moment and it is at this point the young brain metaphorically "lights up." In other words, it makes connections in the brain when new neural pathways are formed.

Best practice: provocations

Cadwell (2003) suggests that through "provocations" (which are resources that are placed into the environment to provoke the children's interest), the place itself then begins to take on new

DOI: 10.4324/9781003309758-9

Figure 8.1 Janos. See video "Janos explores new sights, sounds, and smells" via the QR code

meanings and opportunities for the child. In the film clip, we can see that mum had provided a play opportunity (or learning experience) for Janos which was designed to "provoke" a variety of sensory play experiences.

MARNIE TAKES TURNS WITH ROLLING A BALL

In the film clip (mentioned in Figure 8.2, accessible via the QR code), we meet Marnie who is taking turns to roll the ball! Do take a look as this clip demonstrates the ability of young babies to cooperate with others in the most simple of ways. At just nine months of age, we can see how she imitates the action and understands the need to roll the ball back to Dad. The encouragement she is given results in the repetition of the action.

Figure 8.2 Marnie. See video "Marnie takes turns with rolling ball" via the QR code

Best practice: developing the senses

Infants explore the world through their senses, which allows them to adapt and learn by interacting with their environment. As they take in new information, they connect it to other things they know, and those connections form a structure in the brain. Repetition and practice strengthen these connections, and through "pruning," the unused ones are discarded. It's no wonder then that babies and children appear to enjoy repeating particular actions and why adults should encourage it! Sensory approaches like rhyming, clapping, singing games, and hearing the "beat" in syllables are also important at this age. Babies enjoy repeating the same sounds over and over again as it helps them learn by strengthening the neural connections created in their brain (Blakemore & Frith, 2005).

MARNIE CRAWLS TOWARDS TOY

Now watch the next film clip (mentioned in Figure 8.3, accessible via the QR code) where we can witness the determination of a nine-month-old baby to crawl her way to a desired toy. This is the furthest she has crawled so far. The sheer joy on her face is testimony to the satisfaction gained. As we have seen, brain growth involves building pathways in the brain, and neuroscience has suggested that physical and intellectual activities that are often repeated strengthen these particular neural pathways.

Figure 8.3 Marnie. See video "Marnie crawls towards toy" via the QR code

PAIGE AND A COMFORTER

Judy is grandmother to Paige, who is nearly 12 months old. Why not watch this very short clip (mentioned in Figure 8.4, accessible via the QR code) which was taken after a playful and stimulating time at the zoo. We can see how Judy gently rocks Paige, establishes eye contact, and provides a calming presence. Paige uses a comforter and places her own hand in her mouth to self-soothe. Sleep swiftly followed these actions. Emotional regulation and inhibitory control take years to develop, so babies and young children require ongoing sensitive co-regulated support from those who care for them.

BRAIN AND BODY SENSORY DEVELOPMENT POINTERS

Now we turn to examine child development more generally.

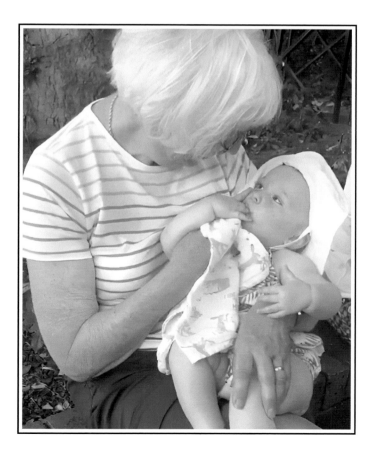

Figure 8.4 Paige and Judy. See video "Paige and a comforter" via the QR code

From around 9 to around 12 months

General brain growth

By around nine months, baby's brain has been busy with rapid growth. In the area of sensory perception, that is, seeing, hearing, feeling, and tasting, multiple neural connections are being made. The first year of life is dedicated to building up these connections and then the "pruning" starts. This is when the brain starts to keep what it sees as useful in life for the baby and to discard what is not going to be helpful. It cannot be overly stressed how much early experiences matter.

General social and emotional development

Around this age, baby starts to recognise more familiar people but may be cautious of strangers. She shows great enjoyment of songs and rhymes and her social time with others during mealtimes.

General physical development

At this stage, her physical skills have progressed significantly. She now sits competently and will make vigorous movements by kicking her legs. She can use an index finger to explore tiny objects and grab any objects within her reach. Baby will turn a toy around to explore and inspect it carefully. Then, around 11 months, she may begin to carry a toy in each hand. Banging toys to make a sound is a favourite activity. Around this age, baby will begin to pull herself up to a standing position using anything around her. She will show excitement by flapping her arms up and down. Around ten months, if something catches her eye, she will attempt to get nearer to reach it! Soon after, around 11 months, crawling may well begin and she may rapidly develop into taking her first steps (for some time, baby may well alternate between crawling or shuffling and taking steps).

General communication and language development

Around this age, baby begins to shout loudly and will attempt a wider range of sounds such as "mm," "gg," "dd," and "brr." She may well understand simple instructions, such as "cuddle teddy."

General cognitive and symbolic development

Baby will show a greater understanding and recognition of daily routines. Around nine to ten months, she also knows more about object permanence (an object continues to exist when it can't be seen); she will reach for an object that is partially hidden, then, a little time later, she will be able to watch a toy being hidden in one place and will then look for it.

PLAY AND PEDAGOGY

Let's turn now to consider how play theory can be the catalyst for enriching a child's development.

Copy me!

Sheridan (1977), when describing the different types of play which can be observed as emerging at particular developmental stages, highlights imitative play as emerging at seven to nine months old. This kind of play is important for a baby in order to learn and put into practice a range of useful ways of functioning in the world. In other words, this imitative play can add to the young child's repertoire of how to say or do things in the world. Dr Kaye, a practising GP and advocate of play (2015), points out that by around 12 months, baby will have a good idea of how some objects in her world might function. For example, she may well know that a hairbrush is something to use on your head. Dr Kaye then describes just how hilarious baby will find it if an adult deliberately uses it in the wrong way.

First-hand experience

Theorists, such as Piaget, Vygotsky, Donaldson, and Dewey, are all in agreement that babies and children really need to experience the world for themselves. This is called "first-hand experience" and is one of the most important principles at the centre of early learning and development.

A magical world

Initially, it seems that babies inhabit a world where objects can just vanish if they are not directly in view. Gopnik, Melzoff, and Kuhl (1999) argue that young babies live in a kind of "magic" world where this happens. It can be described as an "out of sight, out of mind" experience. Later, the baby will search for a hidden toy and this leap in awareness is called object permanence; the baby realises that objects *do* continue to exist even when they cannot see them. According to Gopnik, Melzoff, and Kuhl (1999) in *How Babies Think: The Science of Childhood*, once baby approaches the end of their first year, they can think about familiar people or objects. Then, over the next two years, children begin to build up a picture or narrative about who they are and their place in the world. Inevitably, this internal construction or understanding of who they are has much to do with the child's emotional regulation which is an area of development that will continue to require constant and consistent adult support.

PLAY IT FORWARD

Building on the interesting play research explored above, we can consider a variety of suitable experiences (some of which we have already witnessed in the films).

Practical play-based sensory activities

Name	Description	Age range	Resources	Activity length	Possible brain and body benefit	Safety notes
Crossing the midline	Position attractive new toys/objects so the child has to cross the midline when reaching out to touch them. Place baby on the floor (supported sitting) and have a large safe container in front of her. The toys are positioned on both her right and left sides. Baby can then choose to pick up objects from either side and drop them into a container. Babies can be encouraged to reach across their bodies to pick up a toy on the opposite side and drop the toy into the container	6 months to 5 years	Use toys that babies have not seen before to attract attention and one large safe container or basket	5–10 minutes	Crossing the midline simply concerns the ability to use each limb/eye on both sides of the body Simple activities like this are great for encouraging that area of development	Under general constant supervision
Here I am!	Peekaboo is endless fun and becomes increasingly fascinating for baby – simply hide under a blanket and pop out to say Peekaboo … there you are!	6–18 months	A cloth or blanket for you to hide under	1–2 minutes	Baby can benefit from visual tracking and start to learn about object permanence (and that people still exist even if you can't see them)	Under general constant supervision

Name	Description	Age range	Resources	Activity length	Possible brain and body benefit	Safety notes
Talk to Teddy	Play the "where is …?" game. The adult says: "Where are teddy's ears? Here they are" … and points. Then, hand teddy to baby and say the same and point to the ears Next time … say: "Where is Teddy's mouth?" Point to Teddy's mouth and say: "Here is Teddy's mouth" … and hand teddy to baby and repeat!	6–12 months	A teddy	1–3 minutes	Baby will gradually learn that the sounds they hear adults make are speech and have meaning. Simple activities like this help build up those necessary connections	Under general constant supervision
Listen up	Go on a sound hunt and listen out for leaves scrunching under foot, children laughing, birds chirping, and point these out to baby	6–9 months	No preparation needed When out and about – simply talk to baby about the sounds – then stop and let her see that you are pausing and listening	5–15 minutes	Babies watch our expressions closely and our reaction to new experiences. Discerning between sounds takes time and practice – and fun ways such as this are perfect for the fine-tuning that needs to take place	Under general constant supervision
What's in the hat?	Place some of her favourite toys in lots of different hats or gloves and encourage her to peep inside and pull them out	6–12 months	Old hats and gloves Favourite toys and interesting safe objects placed inside	5–15 minutes	The element of surprise by discovering something for yourself extends to babies – they love to explore and make new discoveries – this activity is perfect for building confidence to make such discoveries	Under general constant supervision

POINTERS FOR DIGGING DEEPER

This is a great opportunity to watch an interesting film (mentioned in Figure 8.5, accessible via the QR code) where Fabia Franco summarises her work with colleagues about infant-directed speech and infant-directed singing. Among other findings, she describes how singing is very popular with a young audience throughout the first year of life.

DISCUSSION STARTERS

- Watch the film clips provided in the last two chapters again and consider how one or two of the activities suggested in the *Practical play-based sensory activities* section might stimulate all-round development for the infants.
- In your opinion, how might first-hand experiences support a young child's sense of developing independence?

Figure 8.5 Dr Fabia Franco. See video "Sing to me!" via the QR code

REFLECTION POINTS

- In the films, the babies demonstrate a variety of reactions to new sensory experiences.
- Playful sensory stimulation weaves a web of rich experiences which delights the developing brain.
- First-hand experiences stimulate the senses and enable the young child to feel empowered.
- Young children begin to learn about how the world works and how to act within it through imitative behaviour.
- Object permanence concerns the developing knowledge that objects and people continue to exist when they are not in sight.

9 Play from around one year to around 18 months

This chapter will introduce you to:

- The theory of the "hidden object"
- The meaning and relevance of "schemas"
- Proximity seeking and what it means for the bonding process
- The way in which objects and play items can be deeply interesting at this stage

JANOS HIDES UNDER A BLANKET (I'M OUT OF SIGHT!)

Do take a little time to watch this fascinating film clip (mentioned in Figure 9.1, accessible via the QR code), where at 12 months of age, Janos (we met him in earlier chapters) is now demonstrating his understanding of how objects and people still exist when they are out of sight. Note how he hides himself under the blanket and finds it very amusing. His mum Holly joins in the fun too.

CHARLIE HIDES UNDER A BLANKET – PEEKABOO!

Now, why not watch the next little film clip (mentioned in Figure 9.2, accessible via the QR code) where at just over 11 months of age, Charlie is also demonstrating his understanding of how objects and people still exist when they are out of sight. There is little doubt that he also finds it amusing!

DOI: 10.4324/9781003309758-10

Figure 9.1 Janos. See video "Janos hides under a blanket (I'm out of sight!)" via the QR code

Figure 9.2 Charlie. See video "Charlie hides under a blanket – peekaboo!" via the QR code

Best practice: children's agency

Judy is Charlie's grandmother and takes an active interest in all of her ten grandchildren and believes it is important for children to have agency in their play. We met Judy in an earlier chapter with another grandchild, Paige. Judy says:

> *Over the years I have learned that any time spent with young children encouraging imaginative play with everyday objects, not specific toys, is so important and I can see how invaluable it is for children to lead the way in their play.*

As we can see from the film with Charlie and many others in this book, spontaneous imaginative play seems to speak to the brain in its language! The brain certainly loves to play.

In this photo, Janos is now 13 months and is trying to see if he will fit into his toy car! At this age, little ones have limited knowledge of spatial awareness.

Figure 9.3 Janos and his schema (repeatable action)

Figure 9.4 Janos. See video "Janos and his ball" via the QR code

At 14 months, Janos is now dedicated to his ball and in later months it becomes the first word he utters. Do watch this film (mentioned in Figure 9.4, accessible via the QR code) and notice his coordination and the drive he exhibits to kick the ball further. At the moment, he is fascinated by things that can go up or down – this is a trajectory schema.

JANOS IS CLIMBING – TRAJECTORY SCHEMA

In this clip (mentioned in Figure 9.5, accessible via the QR code), Janos who is now 15 months old is with dad, who is a professional rock climber. You will see the confidence that his dad has in his son's ability to tackle the wall is almost tangible. Janos exudes physical confidence and the bond and connection between them can be observed. Again, this delightful film demonstrates his interest in things or people who go up or down (a trajectory schema).

Figure 9.5 Janos climbing with dad. See video "Janos is climbing" via the QR code

ETHAN IS SKATEBOARDING – TRAJECTORY SCHEMA

In this fun film clip (mentioned in Figure 9.6, accessible via the QR code), you will see Ethan, who is 17 months, pretending to skateboard, encouraged by his dad, Tom, and his older brother Levi. Being in close proximity to others will remain important for Ethan for some time. Children recognise the safe haven offered to them by others who care for them. In this case, it is his older brother with whom he wishes to be in close proximity as he immerses himself in his latest schema – getting moving!

Figure 9.6 Ethan and Levi. See video "Ethan is skateboarding" via the QR code

ETHAN AND THE SLIDE! – TRAJECTORY SCHEMA

In this next tiny clip (mentioned in Figure 9.7, accessible via the QR code), you will see Ethan coming down the slide as his older brother Levi, who is close behind, remarks how his young brother seems to have no fear! Ethan, similar to Janos who we saw in an earlier clip (mentioned in Figure 9.5, accessible via the QR code), is interested in things or people that go up or down too – this is a trajectory schema.

Best practice: proximity seeking

Proximity seeking is one of the ways in which young children can feel safe. Tom, their dad, says, "Ethan enjoys playing with his older brother Levi and often follows him around. The bond between them is strong."

Figure 9.7 Ethan and Levi. See video "Ethan and the slide!" via the QR code

BRAIN AND BODY SENSORY DEVELOPMENT POINTERS

Now we turn to examine child development more generally.

From around one year to around 18 months

General brain growth

Rapid growth in motor control leads to greater ability to explore – all good for stimulating the brain and making those cognitive connections involved in understanding cause and effect. I do this … and that happens.

General social and emotional development

At this stage, she likes to have a carer close by for security and a favourite comfort toy also offers comfort (a blanket or soft toy can provide a sense of security). Her desire for independence is mounting and her drive to use her senses to better understand the world is beginning to be a source of frustration. She has yet to learn the difference between "me" and "you" and is completely egocentric, which leads the baby to believe that everything "belongs" to her. This is not a demonstration of selfishness – it just means she just has not yet reached the next stage in thinking.

General physical development

By around 12 months, she can sit securely for a long period and can rise to sit from a lying down position. Around this time, she will be able to sit from a standing position and can get up to stand without any support. Feet are usually wide apart, and hands are usually raised to help balance. She may be quite mobile and able to stand for a few seconds and may have already progressed from crawling or bottom shuffling. At this stage she may choose to cruise along furniture and be able to walk without holding on – she may also have already taken her first few steps independently! At this age, she may be able to crawl upstairs. She will tend to throw toys using her whole arm. Pushing and pulling objects is a favourite activity and she will demonstrate increasing agility.

Her fine motor skills are developing fast, and she may well be able to grasp a crayon in a palmer grasp. She is likely to enjoy using a range of mark-making materials. At this age, she can hold her cup or bottle and is able to release a toy deliberately from her hand. She tries to shuffle food onto a spoon and can steer it to her mouth but often misses. She uses a fine pincer grip (grasping an object between the thumb and forefinger) to pick up small objects and, when looking at a book, will turn several pages in one go. Even at this stage, she may begin to show a preference for using one hand in particular.

General communication and language development

Around 12 months of age, baby's first words will be heard, and she will use gestures too. She will frequently imitate words and sounds and will babble tunefully. She may speak two or more recognisable words. You might hear her use just part of the word when trying to communicate something she wants. Her comprehension is developing, and she understands everyday words, such as bath, bottle, and dog. She will also try to join in with conversations. Comprehension precedes articulation: she may well be able to point to parts of her body when asked (e.g., "Where are your feet?"). By around 15–18 months, her interest in books with pictures is developing and she will stare at photos of people's faces.

General cognitive and symbolic development

At this age, she may well draw an adult's attention to things that interest her in the environment, such as objects and toys which are favoured. She can concentrate intently on an object or activity of her own choice for short periods and will demonstrate a developing understanding of what familiar everyday objects can do. She is likely to start to enjoy role-play, perhaps feeding teddy with her spoon or using blankets to cover herself – pretending to go to sleep. The pushing and pulling expertise she is gaining is also providing her with some basic understanding of cause and effect … I pull this toy and it moves. Around this age, she understands simple commands such as "give me the ball" and perseveres when she can't do something, learning through trial and error. At this stage, she is beginning to understand the use of objects and handles them according to their purpose. For example, she knows that a cup is for drinking. She shows delight in pointing at something that catches her eye and makes noises about it.

PLAY AND PEDAGOGY

Let's turn now to consider how play theory can be the catalyst for enriching a child's development.

Play and objects as part of early communication

Dimitrova and Moro (2013; 2015) describe the interactions of parents/carers with toys in a manner which demonstrates to the child the conventional use of those toys. Furthermore, the study directs attention to the importance of the way in which adults encourage the child's object exploration. Piaget (1951) proposed that young children make gains in knowledge about objects in the first two years of life and the use of objects is a significant developmental step. Of course, the use and knowledge of objects is something that can be mutually shared with the parent/carer. The work of Butterworth and Grover (1988) demonstrates that parents' first communications with their child involve physical objects, for example, pointing to a teddy. As Dimitrova and Moro (2013) comment, objects are an essential part of early communication between the infant and parents/carers.

Time spent together is good news

Professor Sam Wass spends much of his time in The Baby Lab at the University of East London, researching how babies learn and respond to their environment. He too believes that humans are social beings and in the earliest of years babies and children do their best learning in social settings. In 2018, he and his team conducted interesting research into how our brains go about supporting this kind of valuable social interaction and what it means in terms of how attentive a baby might be to their environment (Wass et al., 2018). In other words, how more mature brains influence immature brains during social interaction. Their fascinating research using a scalp electroencephalogram (which measures electrical activity of the brain via electrodes fixed to the scalp) recorded brain activity from babies and parents during solo play with toys and during joint play. Their findings suggested that when parents' brains are responding to their babies during social play, the baby is more attentive. This is all good news for parents and carers investing time in playing with their young children.

PLAY IT FORWARD

Building on the useful play research examined above, we can consider a variety of suitable experiences (some of which we have already witnessed in the films).

Practical play-based sensory activities

Name	Description	Age range	Resources	Activity length	Possible brain and body benefit	Safety notes
Off we go …	Playing outside with nature, such as collecting fallen leaves	One year to 18 months	Access to a park in autumn A big canvas bag so baby or you can carry the new "treasures"	5–10 minutes	Play outside demands that children challenge themselves physically and develop more advanced motor skills, such as coordination, balance, and agility	Supervision needed
What is in there?	After baby is 6 months old, put different textured, varying lengths of materials and let baby pull them through a hole in the box	6–18 months	Different textured materials placed inside a cardboard box with a big hole already cut out in the middle	5–10 minutes	Baby will be refining her fine motor skills and her efforts brought about by curiosity will help her understand more about cause and effect – for example, I put my hand in here and I pull out some lovely textured material	Constant supervision, particularly as some of the pieces of material may be quite long

(Continued)

141

Name	Description	Age range	Resources	Activity length	Possible brain and body benefit	Safety notes
Teddy bears' picnic	Sing the *Teddy Bears' Picnic* song as you arrange lots of items on the floor, such as a safe tray, cups and saucers, a blanket to sit on, and a range of cuddly toys	18 months to 3 years	A range of cuddly toys and a tray with toy cups, etc. Blanket to sit on	10–20 minutes	"Let's pretend" activities encourage the use of objects that stand for things in the real world – all good for concept formation	Under general constant supervision
Call me up!	Use a small rectangular cardboard box and pretend to call someone and talk to them. Offer it to baby and see what happens!	18 months to 3 years	A small rectangular box	1–3 minutes	Babies are fascinated by phones and will tend to listen to adults when they speak on them. Playing make believe with a "substitute" object does wonders for the development of imagination	Under general constant supervision

POINTERS FOR DIGGING DEEPER

Proximity seeking

Across all cultures, the benefit of the attachment system is seen to motivate the young child to seek proximity to the parent, especially at times of confusion, danger, or distress, which of course increases the chance of survival. The act of proximity seeking is also used by the young child to internalise the sense of security afforded to them (the adult is a safe haven) and this in turn gives rise to confidence in the young child to explore the world further (often returning to the parent as a safe place). The mother–child discourse (Laible & Thompson, 2000) again highlights the importance of attachment security and the shared positive affect between the mother and child. In fact, proximity (close contact between adult/carer and child) is key to the sharing of an object or toy.

Object(s) toys and "common ground"

Dimitrova and Moro (2013) explore the use of "common ground" associated with objects or toys and parent/carer's communication through gestures. They found that between 8 and 16 months, babies developed common ground knowledge of objects. The "common ground" acts as a way of shaping the way in which parent/carers communicate with their young children.

DISCUSSION STARTERS

- Review the film clips in this chapter that demonstrate schemas and consider which other activities might further tap into the children's current interests.
- Choose five objects that you think might be most interesting and stimulating to this age range.
- How can you ensure that your choice of activities is truly inclusive?
- Young children need a "safe haven" and seek to be in close proximity to those who care for them. What do theorists have to say about the importance of comfort? Further reference: Winnicott, D.W. (1999). *Playing and Reality.* London: Routledge.

Figure 9.8 Curiosity and exploration are key players in brain growth

REFLECTION POINTS

- The beginning of the journey for understanding object permanence can take place through playful interactions.
- Schemas are repeatable actions and, as seen in the film clips, schemas help us understand children's interests and fascinations as they occur.
- Children seek to be near or close to familiar adults (or siblings as seen in the films) who care for them and this can promote a sense of security.
- Adults can introduce relevant and suitable objects or playthings that can help children along their developmental journey.

10 Play from around 18 months to 2 years

This chapter will introduce you to:

- The meaning of "moments of meeting"
- A brief explanation of the "Still Face" experiment
- The joy of reading together
- Experimenting and anticipation can bring laughter
- Why knocking down towers is such fun

MOMENTS OF MEETING WHILE FACE TO FACE

Do watch this delightful film clip (mentioned in Figure 10.1, accessible via the QR code) which shows dad Adrian playing with 22-month-old Jonah. Their closeness while playing is striking. I first spotted them at a local meeting while sitting behind them and observed the natural easy-going relationship they had together, with Jonah content to sit on dad's lap and share the occasional smile or interest in a toy he carried. The following week I plucked up the courage to ask if they would mind being filmed and photographed for this book. Thankfully they agreed. Naomi, our mutual friend (who just happens to be a play therapist), joined us for the little films and even took part. In this film, you will notice the fun of rough and tumble play as Adrian repeats the fun of swinging Jonah up and down. They are both totally absorbed in the play – acknowledging each other, laughing, and making eye contact.

UNDERSTANDING MORE ABOUT MOMENTS OF MEETING

Do take time to watch this short film clip (mentioned in Figure 10.2, accessible via the QR code), where Naomi, a play therapist, describes Daniel Stern's (2004) research about how a child reacts to intimate "moments of meeting." He is a psychoanalyst. The term "moments of

DOI: 10.4324/9781003309758-11

Figure 10.1 Jonah. See video "Jonah and moments of meeting" via the QR code

meeting," is used to describe the way in which quality time or moments have the capacity to bring about a profound sense of mutual connection. Naomi encourages us to notice just how much both the adult and the child shared in the joy of the experience in the earlier film with Jonah and his dad Adrian (mentioned in Figure 10.1, accessible via the QR code).

MOMENTS OF MEETING AND THE "STILL FACE EXPERIMENT"

We are delighted to share with you this film clip (mentioned in Figure 10.3, accessible via the QR code), where we explore the "still face experiment" which was developed by Dr Ed Tronick in the 1970s. It helps us understand how a carer's responses and reactions can affect the

Figure 10.2 Naomi. See video "Naomi talks about moments of meeting" via the QR code

emotional development of a baby. Early in life, infants are learning about other people's reactions to them and how their behaviour can affect others. It is a powerful study which shows our need for social connection from very early in life. We had a go at trying out the "Still Face experiment." Take a look at the film! At first, we can see just how experienced dad is in involving Jonah … enticing him to play – as usually his facial expressions and body gestures are warm and inviting. Then, when dad stopped interacting with him … we can see how sad Jonah felt about the loss of connection.

THE "STILL FACE EXPERIMENT" EXPLAINED

As a follow-up, in this film clip (mentioned in Figure 10.4, accessible via the QR code), Naomi unpacks the understanding of the "still face experiment" which shows us just how important

Figure 10.3 Jonah and dad. See video "Jonah and the 'still face' experiment" via the QR code

human interaction is to a child and how much they crave attention. The sort of interaction shown by dad is vital to a child's emotional and social well-being. Such is the close relationship between them that very quickly we see Jonah's attempts to reinstate the connection. He tries to re-engage his dad by touching his face and moving it.

LAUGHTER BRINGS MOMENTS OF MEETING: LET'S LAUGH!

Let's visit Janos again in this film clip (mentioned in Figure 10.5, accessible via the QR code), where laughter has been a theme of his life so far. Mum, Holly still enjoys sharing in the humour with Janos, who is now 19 months. It seems that the repetition of the sound of the ice dropping, in conjunction with the Jack-in-the-box humour, causes him such hilarity. During this playful exchange, Janos is learning about cause and effect in the most fun way possible!

Figure 10.4 Naomi. See video "The 'still face experiment' explained" via the QR code

Figure 10.5 Janos. See video "Janos seems to say: let's laugh!" via the QR code

While watching other films in this book, you will often be able to spot just how those moments of meeting between child and the carer actually start to happen – look out for what prompts these special times and the connection that is built.

LET'S READ TOGETHER!

This next clip (mentioned in Figure 10.6, accessible via the QR code) features Jonah and his sister Ruby (who has Cerebral Palsy) enjoying a shared book time with Naomi. Note how Naomi encourages participation from both children, acknowledging their need for her attention and responding encouragingly to their communication with her, and she is able to have moments of meeting with both of them!

Figure 10.6 Jonah and Ruby reading together. See video "Let's read together!" via the QR code

READING CAN LIGHT UP THE BRAIN

You will see in this film (mentioned in Figure 10.7, accessible via the QR code) how Naomi describes the way in which Jonah, who is 22 months old, and Ruby both extract something meaningful to them from the experience. They both achieved a moment of meeting with Naomi during that time. Books are very personal and children will take from the activity what *they* need. Research shows that reading regularly with young children stimulates optimal patterns of brain development, which helps build strong pathways in the brain and in turn builds language, literacy, and social-emotional skills that can have life-long health benefits. Recent research led by Dr Hutton at Cincinnati Children's Hospital used functional MRI scans to assess real-time changes in the brains of 19 pre-school children as they listened to stories being read to them. Parents were asked about "cognitive stimulation," including their children's reading habits and how often they were

Figure 10.7 Naomi. See video "Naomi talks about how reading to children helps light up the brain" via the QR code

read to at home. Researchers discovered that reading stimulates the side of the brain that helps with mental imagery, understanding, and language processing and that brain activity, while hearing stories, was higher in the children who were read to at home more often.

EXPERIMENTING WITH SOUND

In this very short film clip (mentioned in Figure 10.8, accessible via the QR code), Jonah experiments with the drum set. Note how he chooses to ignore the offer of drumsticks and prefers to use his hands to make a variety of sounds. He is fascinated and intrigued by the sounds that emerge. This interesting film also demonstrates how children's brains are constantly on the lookout for the "novel." At this stage of development, it is as though we can almost "see" how hard the brain is working (playing!) at making new connections.

Figure 10.8 Jonah. See video "Jonah experiments with sound" via the QR code

EXPERIMENTING WITH "TIMING"!

Do take a look at this next film clip (mentioned in Figure 10.9, accessible via the QR code) where you will see Adrian offering Jonah the joy of knocking down the bricks – their eye contact reveals the shared joke and anticipation of what will happen. It is clearly a joke that they have shared many times. So, what do children benefit from building towers? This sort of play activity helps children with hand–eye coordination. The child has to learn to place the block on the block tower in such a way that does not topple the tower. This encourages spatial awareness and it enhances logical thinking capability. The activity also provides mental stimulation and teaches the child about cause and effect. For example, if the child places the block too close to the edge, the tower topples over.

Figure 10.9 Jonah. See video "All fall down! Where is it?" via the QR code

And, of course, it is all about anticipation of what is about to happen … it is great fun when the bricks all fall down!

EXPERIMENTING AND ANTICIPATION

Now, we turn to visit Ethan again, who is now 18 months and is happily building bricks and then waiting for them to fall down. Do take a look at this film (mentioned in Figure 10.10, accessible via the QR code) where the anticipation on his face is unmistakable … and then he laughs! In the film, you can see the concentration and delight on the child's face.

Figure 10.10 Ethan. See video "Ethan building with bricks" via the QR code

Best practice: provocations

As we can see in these films, play and brain growth appear to be happy companions for each child, as they individually make their way down the winding road of development. The parents in the clips all said that they were keen for their children to explore and investigate their environment through safe play activities. Children engage in symbolic play to understand the world around them (meaning that one object can stand for another, such as in pretend play when children make believe that an object is something else – for example, a broom is a horse). A stimulating environment with lots of play experiences is very important for cognitive as well as social and emotional development. An entry point for empathy can be offered through pretend play – children can try out what it might be like to be someone else and to have a perspective on a situation. Activities like this enable children to practise new emotional vocabulary – all great ways for learning how to get on with others.

BRAIN AND BODY SENSORY DEVELOPMENT POINTERS

Now we turn to examine child development more generally.

From around 18 months to around 2 years

General brain growth

Brain growth involves building pathways in the brain and neuroscience has suggested that (simply put) physical and intellectual activities that are often repeated can help to make the neural pathways stronger.

General social and emotional development

She is now developing a stronger sense of identity and will demand: "me do it." At this stage, she is keen to develop a little independence yet at this time, she is still coming to terms with the very many frustrating things in life, which often gives way to overwhelming feelings. As time passes, with greater support and access to helpful vocabulary, she will learn how to express herself better and frustrations will decrease. She likes to play by herself with an adult close by. During this stage, she will become more aware of others' feelings and will look concerned if she hears another child cry or will seem excited if she hears someone approaching who is using a happy voice.

155

General physical development

At 18 months, she has a strong exploratory impulse and will be curious about everything and will want to "have a go." She starts to walk more confidently, can stop when she wants to without stumbling, and enjoys walking and can carry her toys at the same time. Around this time, she can bend down without falling over and enjoys pushing and pulling large toys. She can climb forward into a chair and then turn around to sit in it. Around 18 months or later, she will start to hold a pencil in her palm or may start to use her thumb and first two fingers in a primitive tripod grasp. She enjoys making dots and can move the pencil up and down and side to side. Around this time, she may also begin to use a paintbrush, using her whole arm to make long strokes.

General communication and language development

Around this age, the young child will love to move her whole body to music she hears. She is likely to be testing out new words she has heard – often muttering them to herself when she is about to fall asleep. At this age, she may start to really enjoy rhymes and will try to join in with actions or sounds. Around this time, she is keen to say "no!" She refers to herself by name, uses around 30 words, and will chatter and jabber. She may also echo the last spoken words of an adult (echolalia) and can even start to put two words together (telegraphese), for example, "Dog come," "More juice." She can respond to simple commands, such as "Give the teddy to me." She may well copy familiar expressions, for example, "Oh dear," "All gone."

General cognitive and symbolic development

Around this time, she is curious and determined to understand as much as possible and happily sits looking at picture books, trying to name objects. She may enjoy placing objects in and out of containers and concentrates on one activity at a time – ignoring everything else.

PLAY AND PEDAGOGY

Drawing on the films in this chapter which demonstrate the interaction between adult and baby, let's turn now to consider how play theory can underpin this understanding.

Problem solving and symbolic play

Young children learn from others not only as models of actions (Bandura, 1986) but also as models of thinking. Adults can help children develop positive behaviours and attitudes by thinking "out loud" and sharing how they problem solve. In nursery or at home where adults behave cooperatively and help each other by sharing problems, the children have an opportunity to observe and subsequently develop the ability to be interdependent and cooperative.

Trawick-Smith et al. (2014) found that toddlers and young pre-schoolers engage in more symbolic make believe with realistic props, whereas older pre-schoolers perform more make believe with non-realistic objects. The TIMPANI five-year project (Toys That Inspire Mindful Play and Nurture the Imagination) found that the impact of a particular toy on children's play is varied and complex according to children's backgrounds and characteristics (Trawick-Smith et al., 2014). There is general agreement that observing children engaging in pretend play is one of the best ways to spot signs of imagination doing its best work. Harris (2000) develops this further by arguing that children as young as two years of age engage in the same level of mental work as adults while engaged in imaginative play. He continues by elaborating on this theory by suggesting that children live with normal expectations of the world but can, as adults do, suspend that reality in order to explore … what if?

PLAY IT FORWARD

Practical play-based sensory activities

Name	Description	Age range	Resources	Activity length	Possible brain and body benefit	Safety notes
Make music	Use music to stimulate exploration with rhythmic movements. Encourage the toddler to play homemade musical instruments in a self-directed way	18 months to 2 years	A range of everyday objects that make interesting sounds (obviously there is a need to ensure baby will not choke or hurt herself on any of the items)	3–10 minutes	Music helps with general development of the brain. For example, it plays a part in increasing the size of the prefrontal cortex. Over time, this means that the brain becomes increasingly good at solving problems, making plans about what to do next, regulating, and identifying emotions. This development is crucial preparation for successful social interactions in the future	Avoid choking hazard–constant supervision is needed with any objects that are not made for purpose
I can tell a story	Children can retell stories in their own way, using items in the story bag	18 months to 5 years	A colourful picture book and safe items from the story, all placed within a soft material bag	5–20 minutes	Children are likely to construct their own narratives as they play with items in the bag – this can help build self-esteem It is also a powerful tool for learning language	None, unless household items are used in place of safe toys

(Continued)

157

Name	Description	Age range	Resources	Activity length	Possible brain and body benefit	Safety notes
My story	Children can start to name familiar people or point to objects using a scrapbook with thick pages, which contains photos of family members, and friends and even their favourite toys	18 months to 5 years	Scrapbook with thick pages Photos of family, friends, and toys	15–30 minutes	Facial recognition stimulates vocabulary and supports children with identifying emotions	Under general constant supervision
Move it	Provide different arrangements of toys and cushions, etc., to encourage crawling, tumbling, rolling, and climbing	18 months to 3 years	Create a challenging but safe obstacle course using toys and soft play materials	10–20 minutes	Support the vestibular system (a sense of movement and balance) through activities that encourage children to move up or down, backwards, or forwards, and around or over	Under general constant supervision
Get digging	Children can find hidden treasure that an adult has hidden in the sand	18 months to 4 years	A sandbox, buckets, spades, a colander or sieves, wooden spoons, and toys to be hidden in the sand	15–30 minutes	Children can explore the different textures They will hear the different sounds that the sand makes as it pours through the variety of containers. Celebrating children's efforts when they search for the items can help build self-confidence	Take care to prevent sand in the hair

POINTERS FOR DIGGING DEEPER

Mirror neurons and their role in social development

The work of Gallese, Eagle, and Migone (2007) acknowledges the importance of the role of neural circuits in social development. They propose that actions and expressions of emotions are similarly activated in another person while they simply watch those actions or emotions. This process is activated by the mirror neuron system. The results of brain imaging experiments (Iacoboni et al.,

1999) using functional magnetic resonance imaging (fMRI) demonstrated that the same parts of the human brain (the inferior frontal cortex and superior parietal lobe) were similarly activated for the person performing a specific action as for the person witnessing the action. This has been defined as the human mirror neuron system. For example, parents have frequently remarked how, if they stick out their tongue at a very young baby, the baby will replicate this action. Since these initial observations were reported by parents, fMRI scans have confirmed that entire networks of neurons have been observed in action. The social cues communicated by a parent who might appear contented, happy, or distressed may elicit a set of similar emotions in the child through the network of neurons as young children are predisposed to learn from these social cues (Rushton, Juola-Rushton, & Larkin, 2010). Of course, these findings have significance for the importance of sensitive adult–child interactions.

DISCUSSION STARTERS

- Watch the film clips again and consider the powerful part played by sheer fun and laughter. How might these playful experiences impact the young developing brain? Why might that be so?
- Consider how Vygotsky and Cole describe movement as preceding perception: "The child resolves her choice not through direct process of visual perception but through movement" (1978: 34). Siegel and Bryson (2012) are quick to point out that research has shown that bodily movements directly affect brain chemistry and provide examples of ways to help children with feelings of overwhelm through physical movements.

REFLECTION POINTS

- Moments of meeting are those times when both adult and child are mutually invested in an activity (as demonstrated in several film clips in this chapter).
- Reading together brings opportunities for children to take what they developmentally *need* from stories.
- The "Still Face" experiment is a powerful demonstration of the way in which our expressions and attention to young children is vital.
- Imagination and symbolic play has rich opportunities for all-round development.
- Laughter is simply a great point of connection for both adult and child.
- Bricks falling down help children to begin to understand cause and effect.

11 Play from around two years to two and a half years

This chapter introduces you to the following:

- The need to behave like a reader
- Schematic play
- The playful nature of the developing brain
- Gender-neutral toys

I CAN READ

Isabella is just over two years old and simply loves her books. Do take a little time to watch this short clip (mentioned in Figure 11.1, accessible via the QR code). You will note how she "behaves like a reader," which is certainly the beginning of building early literacy skills: she knows how the book works; she knows to pause, look, and point at the pictures, "read" the text and then turn the page. She varies her tone as she reads and is clearly satisfied with the narrative as the book concludes. Her confidence is unmissable. Dad filmed her and she was unaware that he was watching. This delightful clip demonstrates the hours that dad has spent reading books with her.

Best practice: provocations

As we saw in this chapter specifically about the brain, studies demonstrate that play is innately attractive to a young child and that there are pathways in the brain that make it so. Rocco, Isabella's dad, says, "I'm fascinated by how a child develops ... having a two-year-old keeps me on my toes ... I feel I am continually trying out different play strategies to see what works for her – every stage is different and I want to invest as much time as possible supporting her play ... and I enjoy it too!"

DOI: 10.4324/9781003309758-12

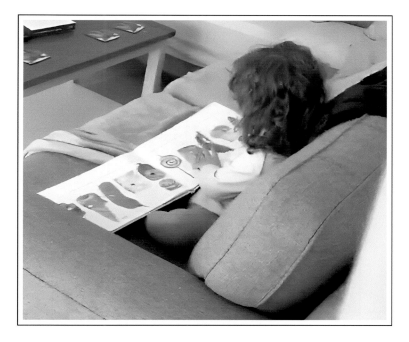

Figure 11.1 Isabella. See video "I *can* read" via the QR code

SCHEMAS AND "LET'S SHOP"!

Let's watch a film clip of Levi (mentioned in Figure 11.2, accessible via the QR code), when he had just turned two and was in Italy visiting his aunt. You will note how keen he is to demonstrate his knowledge of how to shop. Recently, mum said that he has shown a fascination for putting things in and out of containers (this is known as a schema). We can see the intense concentration on his face, oblivious of his surroundings as he confidently places the items on the shopping belt. In this film, it is as though we are witnessing how each thought and every action creates a new connection in the brain which if repeated regularly, forms a new pathway.

Best practice: schemas

Levi's mum says that she enjoys watching her son develop particular interests (schemas) and tries to provide opportunities for him to explore new schemas through child-led play. Recently, she had noticed his particular fascination with putting things in and out of boxes. She knew that these kinds of repeated actions occur as children explore the world around them and as they try to find out how things work.

Figure 11.2 Levi. See video "Let's shop!" via the QR code

It is evident that the "playful" nature of the brain is the main driver in the child's quest for understanding. Athey (2007) suggests that adults should offer children activities linked to schemas which are likely to help sustain interest and further the child's understanding.

BRAIN AND BODY SENSORY DEVELOPMENT POINTERS

Now we turn to examine child development more generally.

From around two years to around two and a half years

General brain growth

Children's brains develop in spurts – one of which occurs around the age of two, with the number of connections between brain cells accelerating fast.

General social and emotional development

Around this age, she likes to play alongside others, and you may witness the start of a desire to join in with others for a fleeting time. She can be affectionate to familiar people in her life but sharing toys can present a real problem to her sense of territory and boundaries. She will tend to waver between being independent and being clingy, expressing her own likes and dislikes, which can lead to tantrums when she gets frustrated. She enjoys playing with objects such as a box and pretending they are something else. She is also likely to be able to part-dress herself with a little help.

General physical development

At this age, she will run safely and may climb stairs confidently, perhaps making a brave attempt at tackling suitable climbing outdoor play equipment. Children around this age enjoy attempting to kick a large ball but might still walk into it. She can throw a ball but can't catch it with any consistent competence. She squats with steadiness and rises to her feet without using hands and continues to enjoy pushing and pulling things on wheels. Around this age, she turns pages in books and picks up small objects, using a fine pincer grasp, and can build a tower of seven or more blocks. Greater hand–eye coordination skill offers more independence in self-help activities and hand preference is more likely now. She can use mark-making tools, such as chubby crayons. She holds a cup with both hands and drinks without much spilling. She may also be able to undo large buttons.

General communication and language development

Around this age, there is usually a growth in enjoyment of songs and rhymes. While playing, you may hear her name people and objects to herself. She is learning words rapidly around this time and may still like to repeat over and over what she has heard someone say (this is called echolalia). She may also begin to ask simple questions of others. She is likely to be able to use action words, such as "go" and "out," and is starting to use pronouns – ("he" and "you") and prepositions ("in" or "on"). She is likely to mistakenly place similar things into the same category, for example, pointing to any four-legged animal and calling it a dog. It is also interesting to hear her ascribe human characteristics to inanimate objects. When adults follow the child's lead in conversation, she will be keen to talk about what she is interested in. When prompted and with a little help, she can give her *age* and full name and can recognise herself in a photo. She is beginning to distinguish between today and tomorrow and is starting to express that concept.

General cognitive and symbolic development

Around this age, she may be able to match colours by finding two bricks the same colour and she may well show you that she can sort objects according to specific characteristics, such as animals or cars. Her imagination is developing fast, and this may open the way for new concerns, for example, she may be worried if a toy is left on its own when she leaves the house. She may begin to understand the consequence of actions, for example, that an object falling over may break. She is likely to delight in understanding and responding to humour. She can now follow simple requests, such as "Please put your bag on the sofa." Her role-play is beginning to evolve and be quite inventive. All the time, she is gaining confidence to try new activities, and with adult support, she will be pleased with her accomplishments.

PLAY AND PEDAGOGY

Drawing on the films in the last few chapters, which demonstrate the playful interaction between adults and infants, let's turn now to consider how play theory can underpin this understanding.

Do take time to watch this interesting film (mentioned in Figure 11.3, accessible via the QR code) about "Parents as Play Partners," which highlights successful ways to support families in providing play activities for their young children. It is an issue that Professor Pat Preedy's work directly addresses. She discusses the need to develop secure attachments and schema-based play through the Parents as Play Partners project. The research was conducted with a range of families with children aged two to three years, in their homes in the United Arab Emirates in (Preedy, Sanderson, & Ball, 2018). The Parents as Play Partners booklet helped parents in their understanding of the importance of play using everyday activities and natural materials. It also highlighted the need to allow the child to lead the play. The results were striking. The quality of engagement and relationship between parents and children after the intervention was impressive and showed enrichment in terms of attachment, language, and thought.

Gender-neutral toys

Cherney and Dempsey's (2010) research discovered that there was a definite difference in which toys children believed were for boys and girls. The defining feature was colour, with the belief that blue indicated toys for boys and pink indicated toys for girls. In conclusion, the research demonstrates that advertisements showing gender toys via colour influence children's choices.

Figure 11.3 Professor Pat Preedy. See video "Let's play together!" via the QR code

Marsh and Bishop's (2013) work, which focussed on analysing playground behaviours, suggested that some forms of play such as "tag" have now become more gender-neutral (more likely to be engaged with by both girls and boys). However, there is still much work to be done to promote equality of opportunity when it comes to accessing gender-neutral play objects.

PLAY IT FORWARD

Building on the interesting play research explored above, we can consider a variety of suitable experiences (some of which we have already witnessed in the films).

Practical play-based sensory activities

Name	Description	Age range	Resources	Activity length	Possible brain and body benefit	Safety notes
Who am I?	Provide a colourful large box that is packed full of items of clothing and musical instruments	2 years to 2 and a half years	Hats, coats, gloves, etc. Large mirror on wall	15–30 minutes	In role-play, children can become whoever they wish – this helps build skills of imagination and creativity – all very helpful skills for future problem solving	Ensure that child does not trip over long clothes
Mountain challenge	Create pathways and "mountains" ... obstacles using soft items such as cushions	2–3 years	Cushions and pillows, blankets and safe foam objects, etc.	10–15 minutes	Physical challenges benefit the development of hand–eye coordination and spatial awareness	Ensure surfaces are safe and maintain supervision
Heuristic basket	Child can explore a range of materials with an adult providing constant attention to ensure the child does not choke on items	16 months to 2 and a half years	A basket which contains a range of natural items, such as shells	10–30 minutes	Offering children the opportunity to explore real objects provokes the confidence to explore the delights of this sensory experience. Heuristic play prompts young children to make their own discoveries and explore the properties of objects (being as creative as they wish in the way they move or combine the items)	Constant vigilance needed from adult
Get splashing	The opportunity to play freely with water is a gift and children need very little incentive to get stuck in	18 months to 5 years	Pots for pouring. A water tray, a waterproof mat, sponges	15–40 minutes	Water play has a calming effect on most children There are opportunities to begin to learn about floating and sinking – the start of scientific understanding	Constant and uninterrupted attention due to drowning hazard

Figure 11.4 The senses are stimulated through play

DIGGING DEEPER

Cultural differences in use and choice of toys

A study by Kim (2002), regarding Korean mothers' behaviours and their personal perceptions in selecting toys for their children, revealed that the longer the child played with toys, the higher value the mother put on the toys in terms of the child's interests in play and developmental appropriateness. Kim (ibid) identified how families from different cultures exert diverse influences on types of play and uses of play materials, and discussed young children's play differences between American and Japanese families. Importantly, Japanese mothers encouraged make-believe play, whereas the United States' mothers preferred children to use more functional toys. The perceived value of toys also varied according to cultural differences, with industrialised societies encouraging toys that purport to enhance cognition (Curtis, 1993). Interestingly, children were found to assign meaning to the toys according to the way in which the adults interacted with the child and the toy.

DISCUSSION STARTERS

- Choose two chapters to read from this reference: Marsh, J. & Bishop, J. (2013). *Changing Play: Play, Media and Commercial Culture from the 1950s to the Present Day: Play, Media and Commercial Culture from the 1950s to the Present Day*. McGraw-Hill Education. In your view, how has "commercialism" impacted the play landscape over the last 20 years?
- Watch the film clip with Levi and his shopping experience again and consider how important it is to ensure that all children have the opportunity to be empowered and have agency. How can we ensure that a young child's current interests are respected?

REFLECTION POINTS

- As delightfully demonstrated in the film with Isabella, young children relish the opportunity to behave like a reader as this instils confidence in the development of essential literacy skills.
- Schemas are repeatable actions and are a real source of learning about the world as shown by the film clip of Levi and his shopping experience.
- Gender-neutral toys are important for children to broaden their ideas about how the world works and not to be limited by stereotypical expectations.

12 Play from around two and a half years to three years

This chapter introduces you to the following:

- Imaginary play
- The strength of emotions at this age
- Bruner's theory
- Strides in language development around this age
- How creative play supports brain and all-round development

SAND AND ICE-CREAM – IMAGINATION DOES ITS WORK

Mona is mum to three children under five and as a senior lecturer in education and module leader for play and pedagogy, she is passionate about her children getting the very best out of every moment of play. In this fascinating film clip (mentioned in Figure 12.1, accessible via the QR code), her youngest son, Rami, who is two years old, is playing with his friends Kamilah, six years old, and Adnan, who is five. Together, they were playing with kinetic sand and … when the children started to design ice-creams, Mona spotted an opportunity to enhance the play and quietly popped real ice-cream cones into the mix. This short clip shows the children's total immersion, belief in their play, and genuine conversations – all of which are fascinating – even the playful tussle over resources that ensues!

Best practice: provocations

Two-year-olds are detectives of the highest order – searching the world for clues about how it works. This is the age of great curiosity. The world can be a very exciting place – everything is new, objects need to be explored, and the drive to learn is evident in the way children of this age play.

DOI: 10.4324/9781003309758-13

Figure 12.1 Rami. See video "Sand and ice-cream!" via the QR code

There are endless possibilities afforded to children when they wholeheartedly enter an imaginary space and this relates to the development of self-regulation and future problem-solving skills. The brain is known to be particularly absorbent at this stage; researchers discuss this propensity as "neuroplasticity."

Rami's mum, Mona, says, "The world seen through the eyes of a two-year-old, is a playground ripe to be investigated – I simply watch the child for clues … for ways I can just offer an extension to their detective work and look for ways to seed the play environment."

"LET ME CHOOSE" – CHILDREN'S RIGHTS

Do take a look at this very short film (mentioned in Figure 12.2, accessible via the QR code) where you will see Charlie again (we met him and his grandmother Judy in an earlier chapter). In this film,

Figure 12.2 Charlie. See video "Let's dance" via the QR code

he is nearly three years old now. He loves to be creative and enjoys dancing. He is wearing mum's tutu. Judy, his grandmother says, "I feel it is important for my grandchildren to engage in whatever play activities they choose."

Best practice: rights of the child

It is important to challenge all our thinking around sexuality, gender-typical behaviours, and ensure that children grow up to believe and understand that everyone has rights. Do take time to seek out and read the work of Bhana and Mayeza (2016). This is a particularly helpful piece of reading to deepen your understanding.

BRAIN AND BODY SENSORY DEVELOPMENT POINTERS

Now we turn to examine child development more generally.

From around two and a half to around three years

General brain growth

Brown and Jernigan (2012) remark on the consistent theme of fast-changing and significant architectural "blossoming" in the brain in the early years – leaving us with little doubt that the brain particularly likes to play during this period!

General social and emotional development

At this age, she still possesses a strong sense of self and can be quite possessive of toys and space with even greater conviction about expressing her own likes and dislikes. She may build a special friendship with another child, and will try to help or give comfort when others are distressed. At this stage, she is still learning about separation from her main carer for short periods of time and at times will seem to manage it with ease, while at other times it can be a challenge. She is likely to be seen to engage in play with one or two particular children, either entering their play (temporarily) or seeming to invite others to join in – but this is not yet truly cooperating as each one is really still playing with their own toys or engaging in their own experiences.

General physical development

You may see her balancing for several seconds while standing on one foot and be able to stand on tiptoe. The young child can now climb with determined confidence and may enjoy using the pedals of a pedal toy to propel themselves along. With a significant development in her fine motor skills, more intricate tasks are appealing and less frustrating. Around this time, she may attempt more sophisticated activities, such as bead threading. She is likely to enjoy making circular shapes and lines with her fingers in paint and sand, copying simple shapes you draw or building a tower of eight or more blocks. At times, she may like to join in fully with action songs.

General communication and language development

Around this age, the young child will listen with interest to any exciting noises and expressions adults make when they read stories, such as the mooing of a cow. She will be learning new words rapidly and will attempt to use them when talking to others. Around this time, she is likely to start to ask: "what?" "when?" and "who?" which will further both her understanding and vocabulary. With the increase in understanding of a vast number of words (around 1,000 – more than they can pronounce), she is fast becoming an efficient conversationalist! She may now begin to use "I," "me," and "you" correctly.

General cognitive and symbolic development

Around this age, she will begin to understand more about cause and effect, for example, if she knocks a bowl over, the contents will spill out. She is likely to point out more detail in a book and will search for a favourite character or animal. She will attempt a jigsaw with three or four large pieces with more confidence. Using simple words, she will have a go at conveying the location of an object, for example, "The toy box has my teddy in it." She is beginning to organise and categorise objects, for example, placing all the teddies and cars in separate piles.

PLAY AND PEDAGOGY

Drawing on the films in this chapter which demonstrate how sensitive observations of children's interests are the best place to start, let's turn now to consider how play theory can underpin this understanding.

Effective communication between the young child and adult appears to work well when both have an interest in the object, toy, or play activity. This shared interest acts as an effective anchor for playful communication to follow. Due to the efficacy of the bonding and attachment process, mostly parents appear to naturally support their child's efforts. These efforts are well established as the act of "scaffolding" (Bruner, 1983).

So, what did Bruner say about play and how an adult can support children while they play? In this film clip (mentioned in Figure 12.3, accessible via the QR code), Naomi explains how Bruner, like Vygotsky, emphasised the social nature of learning through the process of scaffolding. Both theorists agree that adults should play an active role in assisting the child's learning. Do take time to notice how in many of the films in this book, you can see the way in which the adults go about scaffolding the children's play and how they respond to this sensitive guidance.

Emotions and the brain

Around this age, it seems that childhood is filled to the brim with emotions. Young children swing from one emotion to another very easily and often need support "grounding" themselves

Figure 12.3 Naomi. See video "Bruner's theory" via the QR code

(functional adaptation to the experiences in the environment). Sensitive and generous support given to the young child experiencing huge emotions can coax the developing brain into better self-regulation and more beneficial problem solving (higher order thinking).

Mutually beneficial synchronous exchanges

Although much research about synchronous exchanges has focused on babies (as highlighted by Harrist & Waugh, 2002), it has been shown that when the child reaches two to three years of age where they possess increased mobility and cognitive ability, then the communication between the child and carer moves from pre-verbal to verbal. This all paves the way for even more synchronous exchanges which begin to emerge as a dialogue akin to that of adult to adult. These synchronous

Figure 12.4 Older siblings can help to "scaffold" play too

exchanges are again mutually beneficial. The significance of these synchronous exchanges and shared experiences (including mutual play with toys) is an exciting area ripe for future study.

Hart and Risley (2003) found that the language development of a child at two years was closely correlated to the way in which carers or parents conversed with their baby right from birth. Of course, for young children being able to communicate how they feel – their needs, fears, and desires – is a big step forward in childhood.

PLAY IT FORWARD

Building on the interesting play research examined above, we can consider a variety of suitable experiences (some of which we have already witnessed in the films).

Practical play-based sensory activities

Name	Description	Age range	Resources	Activity length	Possible brain and body benefit	Safety notes
Matching pictures and photos	Use strong card onto which you stick photos of items in the real world. The challenge is for the children to find them in the room and place them on a tray	2 and a half years to 3 years	Tray Photos taken and printed and stuck on a card	20 minutes	Ability to link picture (visual representation) with objects in the real world	None other than general constant supervision
Look and say	Play a game of point and say – look and find. The children gather up as many objects as they can (according to a particular colour) and place them on a tray or a table	2–5 years	Take a selection of items from around the room (toys and safe real objects of a certain colour) and hide them	10–20 minutes	Games such as this encourage language development and visual discrimination	Under general constant supervision
Build a den	Offer children lots of old material to make their own den	2 and a half to 4 years	Pillows, blankets, netting – and items to secure them to, such as two chairs		Setting up provocations following children's interests enables adults to build on a child's natural and individual curiosity Younger children will play solo and enjoy working on their "enclosure schema"! Older children playing together towards a common purpose in an activity like this tend to develop skills of negotiation, debate, teamwork, cooperation, and persuasion	Under general constant supervision and ensuring the den does not collapse on them

Name	Description	Age range	Resources	Activity length	Possible brain and body benefit	Safety notes
Who am I?	Challenge children to dip into the bag and choose a card with an animal on it. Then they place the card face down on the floor and pretend to be that animal without telling you what it is. Can you guess? Each child takes a turn	2–5 years	A large bag full of cards of different pictures of animals	10–15 minutes	Pretending to be an animal challenges children to be creative in the way they express their ideas	Under general constant supervision
Cardboard box challenge	Lots of things can be made out of cardboard boxes. The child will have their own ideas, such as making a house, a car, or a boat. They might like to colour it in too	2 and a half to 4 years	Range of cardboard boxes, colouring pencils or crayons	15–40 minutes	Children need the freedom to create their own play opportunities. This activity is a catalyst for open-ended and child-led play which can help boost the development of problem-solving and self-regulation skills	Look out for any split parts of the box and sharp edges

POINTERS FOR DIGGING DEEPER

Shared play

Researchers are discovering that there are multiple benefits to be gained for both the child and the adult while playing in harmony. Researchers tend to speak about something called "higher triadic synchrony." This simply describes those delightful moments that occur as a result of close physical proximity for parent and child. Perhaps most significantly, it triggers lower cortisol levels (Gordon & Feldman, 2008). There are important causal associations to be made between the neurobiological basis of bonding and synchrony and shared play between adult/parent/carer and young children around their use of a shared object or toy.

So what might be the reward to the adult and child when playing in this manner?

Feldman and Eidelman (2007) have established that maternal behaviour increases OT receptor binding in brain areas central for parenting (in other words, parents derive a reward from their young infant). This process is known as the oxytocinergic system responsible for the attachment and bonding process, which acts as a bio-behavioural feedback loop. In other words, this positive process seems to have a "bounce back" effect. The "positioning" of the object/toy as a possible mutually beneficial driver between an adult/carer and young child may well contribute to the bonding process but this is an area which is under-researched.

What about fathers in particular?

Furthermore, research regarding the neuroendocrine basis of fathering and the links between paternal behaviour and the oxytocinergic system is in its early stages (Feldman & Eidelman, 2007). However, there are indicators that interaction between father and infant (often in overt playful ways) may in simple terms shape the neuroendocrine system (Feldman & Eidelman, 2007).

DISCUSSION STARTERS

- Think back to the films already viewed and consider the importance of materials which don't have a specific outcome, such as sand, clay, or an empty cardboard box. Consider each area of child development and make a note of how an open-ended activity might provide suitable support.
- Now consider a different activity. Perhaps choose one from the suggested activities above and consider how a young child might be supported through adult encouragement (scaffolding) to take their next step in understanding how the world works.

REFLECTION POINTS

- Adults have an important role to play in observing children's play and responding sensitively as we have seen in the film with Rami in this chapter.
- There is an interesting link between imagination and neuroplasticity which emphasises the need for rich child-initiated play opportunities.
- Sensitive adult support during times of overwhelming emotions at this stage can help children with self-regulation and future problem-solving skills.
- The act of "scaffolding" is a thoughtful way to enhance a sensory experience.

13 Play from around three years to four years

This chapter will introduce you to:

- Children's rights in relation to play
- The need to challenge gender-stereotypical play
- Children's rights to wallow in play and dream and imagine
- The importance of ensuring diversity and inclusion in children's play
- The joy of role-play and meaning of the "theory of mind"
- Creative play and its link to mental health and well-being

MIRRORED SELF: CHILDREN HAVE A RIGHT TO PLAY

In this impressive film clip (mentioned in Figure 13.1, accessible via the QR code), Ishy, who is three years old, is dipping into his favourite box full of old hats, gloves, and clothes. With a hat firmly placed on his head and a wooden spoon in hand, he starts an elaborate dance with his mirrored self. His rhythm and coordination are as mesmerising as I am sure the play felt to him. His growing smile indicates the pleasure this gave him as he tries to view himself from various angles! His mum, Mona, caught him on camera. Do take a look at this clip as it demonstrates that with the simplest and cheapest play accessories, children will find unique play opportunities.

Best practice: children's agency

Mona says,

> This little clip shows just how much we can trust children and accept that their play ideas are going to meet their needs for that particular time in their lives. I like to see myself as a "play partner" and strive to be an efficient observer – at times, I'm just on the outskirts of their play – proffering an object or two … that just might be the icing on the cake for their play experience.

DOI: 10.4324/9781003309758-14

Figure 13.1 Ishy. See video "Mirrored self" via the QR code

The use of "loose parts" in play is increasingly becoming recognised as a valuable resource in early years learning environments. In short, this includes the use of loose, tactile-based materials. The important point is that they must be versatile. That way, children can adapt them and take a lead in how they can be used. Here are just a few suggestions: boxes, blocks, pipes, buckets, crates, sheets, and small rocks, stones, shells, sticks, and leaves. Of course, they make perfect sense for use with mathematical activities, such as size and shape. Gibson, Cornell, and Gill (2017) found that early indications from existing research on children's cognitive, social, and emotional development looked promising but more research was needed.

VROOM … OFF GO THE CARS: CHILDREN HAVE A RIGHT TO PLAY IN THE WAY THEY CHOOSE

Do watch this lovely film clip (mentioned in Figure 13.2, accessible via the QR code) where Isabella is finding car parking spaces for her fleet of toy cars. Clearly, she relishes the shared experience of playing with her dad.

Figure 13.2 Isabella. See video "Vroom … off go the cars" via the QR code

Best practice: children's rights and building bonds in play

Isabella's dad says,

> I love playing imaginary games with my daughter, it helps me destress and when I get lost in her world of play it feels like we're connecting on a deeper level and strengthening the bond between us as father and daughter. I can see by the smile on her face and how it lights up that she's enjoying my time with her and when we're creating new narratives together it does wonders for my well-being. It's like being a kid again. It's the best remedy for when I've had enough of sending emails and feeling weighed down by the stresses of work. I try to use any old household items or her toys to encourage imaginative play but sometimes if we're outside we have nothing but the outdoor elements to improvise with, like sticks and leaves. I've learnt that I have to throw myself into it otherwise she senses I'm not in the mood, but when I fully commit into her world of play, I reap the benefits.

HANA READS TO THE DOG: CHILDREN'S AGENCY IN ACTION

Do take a little time to watch this next film clip (mentioned in Figure 13.3, accessible via the QR code), where Hana has a captive audience as she practises her skills of reading to the class!

Figure 13.3 Hana. See video "Hana reads to the dog" via the QR code

Her bold and confident reading is a delight to observe. Her comfortable body language suggests that this is a familiar activity which she enjoys. She is bilingual. As we saw in an earlier chapter in the film with Isabella, she is learning to behave "like a reader" and this is crucial for her confidence.

Best practice: children's rights

Around this age, children will tend to verbally label themselves as girls or boys and begin to play with stereotyped toys (Shaffer, 2009). The early years foundation stage (EYFS) seeks to promote sound equality of opportunity and anti-discriminatory practice: explaining that it is every child's

Figure 13.4 Books can light up the brain with imagination!

right to be included and supported. It also explains that through positive and affirmative adult modelling, they can learn how to look after their bodies.

It is very important to challenge these gender stereotypes and to encourage girls as well as boys to reach their full potential by not limiting their choices. Lourdes says,

I ensure that children have equal access to all play materials as this guards against gendered behaviour so that children can grow up to be whoever they dream to be. And, I challenge any form of racism in my nursery.

CHILDREN HAVE A RIGHT TO WALLOW IN PLAY

In this very short film clip (mentioned in Figure 13.5, accessible via the QR code), the need to allow children to engage their senses and simply wallow in play is beautifully described by

Figure 13.5 Sid. See video "Children can wallow in play" via the QR code

Sid Mohandas, a Doctoral researcher at Middlesex University and a former Montessori educator and teacher trainer.

NEURODIVERSITY AND CHILDREN'S RIGHTS

Here is an opportunity to watch this very personal film (mentioned in Figure 13.7, accessible via the QR code), where André Skepple, founder of FullSpektrum Ltd, discusses his own educational and neurodevelopmental challenges which motivated him to explore the use of science and technology to improve the lives of neurodivergent children, young people, and adults with Special Educational Needs and Disabilities (SEND). Neurodiversity simply means the way in which human minds differ and is an overarching term for all types of brains: neurotypical and neurodivergent brains.

Figure 13.6 Children have a right to imagine and dream. Picture books capture imagination and transport children into another world

Figure 13.7 André Skepple. See video "Neurodiversity" via the QR code

Best practice: celebrating identity and children's rights

Michelle De Leon, who is the founder and Chief Executive Officer of World Afro Day, a global day of change, education, and celebration of Afro hair and identity, explains that it is important to help children learn about their differences and celebrate identity from a young age. She points out that many educators are discovering this through the Little and Big Hair Assembly events and resources.

Michelle says:

There's such a joy and power for all children exploring hair through World Afro Day. Since the government and EHRC recently recognised Afro hair equality as an important focus, we hope more teachers will embed this into their curriculums and calendars. Afro hair inclusion can boost many subject areas like STEM, history, art, music and literacy, creating more inspirational content for children. Learners have used language like "unstoppable" and "superpower" to describe the impact that our work has on them. Learning to love the human race in all its diversity is education for life.

Figure 13.8 Michelle de Leon

ADDRESSING RACISM IN THE EARLY YEARS

Researchers, such as Boutte, Lopez-Robertson, and Powers-Costello (2011), highlight concerns around how young children internalise racist messages.

- During play how might adults address racism in their setting and respond to any racism in young children's play?
- What further research is needed to identify strategies for adults working in settings to ensure they demonstrate inclusive practice?

BRAIN AND BODY SENSORY DEVELOPMENT POINTERS

Now we turn to examine child development more generally.

From around three to around four years

General brain growth

By three years of age, the significant gains in cognitive and symbolic development can be attributed to a child's natural enthusiasm to explore the world. The brain has around 1,000 trillion brain connections (synapses). The greatest changes in areas of the brain are occurring within higher order cortical regions such as the prefrontal cortex.

General social and emotional development

Around this age, her need for independence is gaining importance and is crucial for ongoing confidence. She is really starting to enjoy helping adults who are in her life and shows more affection to younger children. At this stage, she is better at expressing her feelings with words which can lessen her frustrations in life. She is now beginning to play cooperatively and is more willing to share and take turns. She believes that all rules are fixed and can be quite adamant about this aspect of play! She can play more imaginatively which can, in turn, lead to the development of fears.

General physical development

Physical prowess is developing, and she will enjoy jumping from a low height, walking in different directions (backwards and sideways), and crawling through apparatus. Around this age, she will demonstrate an improved sense of coordination and balance and will run skilfully, negotiating space successfully and adjusting speed or direction to avoid obstacles. She can throw and catch a ball and may be able to use pedals on tricycles (moving around with better spatial awareness). She can stand and walk on tiptoes, balance on one foot, and kick a ball. She can draw a person: first, the body, then the legs, then arms coming out of the head. She may be able to hold a pencil more effectively to make marks and shapes on paper with a crayon, although she may not yet have a dynamic tripod grasp. She can build towers of nine or ten bricks and can make up and down and circular movements using pencils, paintbrushes, and sticks in mud. She is beginning now to learn how to use safety scissors and can use a fork and spoon at mealtimes.

General communication and language development

Around this age, you will notice that she can hold simple conversations. She is truly trying to understand the world better and will frequently ask: "why?" Her listening skills will improve rapidly provided she is listened to patiently. Please note that around this time she may stutter when very excited or nervous. Her vocabulary is likely to be impressive as she now knows and can say up to several hundred words and can link three or four words together in a sentence (although missing out words such as "and," "the," and "is"). She may well start to use verbs, such as "run," "eat," and adjectives, such as "small." Around this age, when speaking, she will show that she understands and uses the singular and plural in the right way. When playing with other children, they will tend to use a mixture of gesture, the odd word, or broken sentence – but still understand each other quite well.

General cognitive and symbolic development

Around this age, certain books become favourites, and she will ask for them to be re-read time and time again. So, she will listen to stories that are meaningful to her and will even start to be able to remember favourite parts. When something attracts her attention, she will listen to other children and adults. At this age, children enjoy imaginative play and role-play and malleable materials. With a developing sense of humour, she delights at making others laugh. At the same time, she can also be strong willed and competitive. She is likely to enjoy learning new skills and be ready for the challenge offered through more complicated jigsaw puzzles and digital games. She can control her own attention when playing – stopping and starting at will. At this stage, she is beginning to get a sense of the difference between present and past and may understand a little more about how the seasons and weather change. She will often confuse fact and fiction and might insert an "event" from a story into an event in her own life when recalling a situation. Around this age, she will be starting to count from one to ten but may yet not truly understand that one number equals one object. She can also sort objects into simple categories and match three primary colours.

PLAY AND PEDAGOGY

Drawing on the films in this chapter (particularly the clip with Ishy), let's turn now to consider how theory can deepen understanding of the value of specific play opportunities.

Role-play

Sociodramatic play, otherwise known as role-play, is well established as a type of play that offers the young child significant gains in terms of cognition, language, and social competence (Fisher, 1992). Several studies, such as Lillard et al. (2013), found that self-regulation skills also increase during pretend play. This premise has obvious consequences. For example, when children engage in pretend play with others, there are always rules to be negotiated between them. Frequently, role-play also involves an element of a shared understanding that one object might represent something else. This is symbolic thought – in other words, one thing can stand for another. When young children are immersed in imaginative play of this nature (where they are pretending that a toy or something can stand for another, such as a box could be a ship), they are reaping significant benefits in terms of language, both in terms of what the child comprehends and the words they choose to use (Lewis et al., 2000).

Theory of mind

Theory of mind is an interesting concept which concerns the human capacity to understand that others have thoughts, beliefs, and feelings that may be the same or different to you. The word "theory" is now understood by some researchers as to be slightly misleading since the process actually starts off not as a theory but as a mechanism. According to Leslie, Friedman, and German (2004), the "theory of mind" mechanism is part of the core architecture of the human brain, which specialises in learning about mental states.

This ability to consider someone else's perspective certainly does not occur suddenly – it is a gradual understanding which typically becomes more apparent to others around 4–5 years of age. Even then, developmentally it is not as straightforward as it might seem. There are many factors involved, which are explored by researchers such as Bellerose, Beauchamp, and Lassonde (2011). What most researchers agree upon is the fact that the roots of empathy draw on the developing skill of being able to sense what it might be like to walk in someone else's shoes.

What might happen if ...

Walker and Gopnik (2013) and Buchsbaum et al. (2012) suggest that pretend play provides oppor-tunities for children to think through step-by-step "what might happen if ..." scenarios. This offers the child preparation for strategic thinking about how things *might turn out*. Furthermore, it all helps out in terms of beginning to regulate any unwanted impulses that might inhibit a desired goal, such as unwanted conflict with others.

Creativity and imagination

Vivian Gussin Paley proposes that a child's development is impacted by stories. In her book, *A Child's Work* (2004), she discusses the role of fantasy play for early years practitioners. Paley developed ways in which play can be used to encourage imagination. Playing in a creative and imaginative way is a neurological process, which means that it involves both the brain and the body's nervous system (Churches, Dommentt, & Devonshire, 2017). The profound impact of play is a sequence of significant action and reaction and has a well-established positive link to health and well-being.

Here is an opportunity to watch a very short film clip (mentioned in Figure 13.9, accessible via the QR code), where Angela, an experienced mental health practitioner, explains why she is passionate about every child's right to play and the way in which it can support their well-being and self-esteem.

Figure 13.9 Angela. See video "Play supports children's mental health" via the QR code

Figure 13.10 The brain loves to have the freedom to "join the dots" through play

PLAY IT FORWARD

Practical play-based sensory activities

Name	Description	Age range	Resources	Activity length	Possible brain and body benefit	Safety notes
Treasure hunting	Encourage her to explore the outdoors by setting up a treasure hunt challenge. Children can hunt for particular objects which are shown on cards, find them and put them in a bag. At the end, they use their own words to describe the treasures they have found	3–5 years	Safe canvas bag Cards with pictures of objects to find	20–30 minutes	The ability to link up words we say with pictures (and real items) is an essential step towards understanding how language really works. Also, the added challenge of finding the objects seen on the cards and then using words to describe the objects helps embed the process further	Beware of poisonous plants and other unsafe objects. Keep close by while the child searches for treasure

Name	Description	Age range	Resources	Activity length	Possible brain and body benefit	Safety notes
Musical challenge and dance routines	Offer musical challenges using objects from around the room such as a pot to use as drums and a rice shaker. Then, encourage the child to make up crazy dance routines	3–5 years	Gather together objects that are safe to strike and shake and hit Provide a makeshift "stage" – even just a blanket on the floor can symbolise a "stage" and a few chairs make up the audience!	20–30 minutes	Musical challenges help a young child's body and mind work together. Dancing to music helps with self-expression too	Use only objects that will not break
My own library	Take the young child to the library and enjoy looking at books together. Back at home, collect up all the books you can find and create a "library" using stacks of boxes to make shelves full of books	3–5 years	Trip to the library Boxes to act as makeshift shelves Lots of books Comfy place to sit	10–20 minutes	A love of books is developed over time as children realise that they contain a wealth of information and delight. The link between words and pictures also takes time. Playing at "library-time" can help foster a love of books	Under general constant supervision
Puppet show	Make sock puppets and put on a puppet show	3–5 years	Old socks Felt for face features Safe adhesive Two chairs and a blanket to be made into a puppet theatre	10–20 minutes	Fun activities like this help to boost the development of problem-solving and self-regulation skills. They also foster imagination	Under general constant supervision

POINTERS FOR DIGGING DEEPER

Children's rights and the need to listening carefully

Adults who have taken the time to really *hear* what children have to say will testify to incredible words of wisdom, insight, and humour that have come from the mouths (or through the body language) of even the youngest child. While that may be fascinating, probably the most important point for us as adults is to note that the views of young children, their aspirations, hopes, and dreams *must* be heard. It is also worth considering the value placed on listening to children in The United Nations Convention on the Rights of the Child, and the 1989 Children Act, which requires that children's views be taken seriously.

Of course, when children are very young, their language is not sufficiently developed to convey exactly what they want to tell us. So, being alert to what they want to say in other ways becomes very important. Children need plenty of encouragement to communicate. This requires time and space to be heard.

The art of powerful conversation

There is no doubt that children learn to develop good listening skills if they are listened to by adults who show real interest in what they are saying. So, what do children really want to talk about? It is fundamentally about tuning into a young child's perspective on the world. I have always found that *genuine* conversation, even with the under-twos, works for me. If I am not really sharing in the conversation, just firing questions at them – it grinds to a halt very quickly. However, if I talk about my own experiences and build on what they are talking about, the conversation takes off. For example, I remember having a meaningful conversation with a three-year-old about our experiences in the snow. This child talked about how it felt when she walked on the crunchy snow in her boots, and I contributed my experience of making snowballs the day before. We took it in turns to talk and exchange feelings and opinions; this is true conversation.

DISCUSSION STARTERS

How essential are verbal and non-verbal feedback and how might they impact children's rights?

Try this test: sit another adult down and ask them to pay little, if no attention, to what you are going to tell them for the next five minutes. Then, start to tell this person about the most exciting day of your life. You are likely to find that it is difficult to keep up any enthusiasm or determination to keep going for the whole five minutes! Now, if we as adults need some reassurance and

194

acknowledgement for what we say, how much more might children need attention and constant reassurance to communicate their thoughts and ideas (especially at a time when they are only just developing their linguistic skills)? Perhaps consider how difficult it is to converse in another language: learning another language as an adult is hard enough and to keep a conversation going in this new language – without helpful prompts and encouragement – can quickly bring the communication to a halt!

- Choose a film clip to view again from any of the previous chapters and consider why non-verbal communication is important by debating the following paragraph:

  Adults can discover the views of young children and the way to success seems to be in treating children as "experts" in their own lives. Allowing children to express themselves non-verbally can tell us a lot about what goes on in their lives. There is no doubt that music is an effective way to communicate with children – sometimes we all can feel "lost for words," and it can allow us to express our innermost feelings. Thinking again about the film clip with Ishy and his music, discuss how musical activities can be inclusive in a specific situation, such as within the home environment or in a nursery.

REFLECTION POINTS

- Children have a right to high-quality play experiences.
- All the film clips in this chapter and previous ones have emphasised the need for children to be supported to become active participants in their play as it boosts self-esteem and belief in their own capabilities.
- Loose parts play has much to offer children developmentally.
- There is a need to combat gender-stereotypical play.
- Ensuring diversity and inclusion in high-quality play for children is vital for their well-being.
- Role-play (also known as sociodramatic play) offers multiple developmental benefits to the young child, such as in the area of language, symbolic thinking, and developing social skills.
- "Theory of mind" is the gradual process of understanding that others have thoughts and feelings, which at times may be similar, and at other times may be different to our own. Understanding another person's perspective is the basis of empathy.
- Creative play is known to have a link to positive mental health and well-being.
- Non-verbal communication is the way in which we start to communicate right from birth and must be valued throughout childhood and beyond.
- Children's rights are paramount.

14 Play from around four years to five years plus

This chapter will introduce you to:

- The joy of immersion in play
- Digital play
- The value of outdoor play
- Creative play
- Play-based learning and the Early Years Foundation Stage
- Pedagogical approaches

LEYLA IS FAMOUS – IMMERSION IN PLAY

Do watch this intriguing film clip (mentioned in Figure 14.1, accessible via the QR code), where Leyla is sprawled out on the floor, relaxing with an iPad in front of her. In this short clip, we see how she enters an imaginary space where she has an audience and is busy making a film of herself for the viewer. The depth of her immersion in the play is impressive.

LEVI GETS GARDENING – IMMERSION IN PLAY

We met Levi in an earlier chapter with his younger brother, Ethan. In this delightful film clip (mentioned in Figure 14.2, accessible via the QR code), we see Levi in his great-grandmother's garden. She has assigned a special place for him to explore gardening. Levi takes the responsibility of watering the plants seriously – he is totally engrossed and in control of the activity. His grandmother, observing his desire to seek out minibeasts, offers him a magnifying glass. As we have seen in recent brain studies mentioned earlier, for the young child each thought and every action generated through play creates a new connection in the brain. A new pathway in

DOI: 10.4324/9781003309758-15

Figure 14.1 Leyla. See video "Leyla is famous!" via the QR code

Figure 14.2 Levi. See video "Levi in his grandparent's garden" via the QR code

the brain is formed if it is repeated on a regular basis; in other words, it becomes the chosen route. For Levi, playing in his great-grandmother's garden has become familiar territory and the popular phrase "neurons that fire together, wire together" is an emerging reality for his neural development.

Best practice: outdoor spaces

Levi's great-grandmother recognises the potential of the outdoor learning environment, and as someone who has worked with children most of her life, her passion has never diminished. She says, "A great outdoor space offers children the opportunity to be in charge of the investigation. There are places where they can be quiet and calm and others where they can be as loud and boisterous as they wish." Her views are very much in alignment with Professor Jan White (2019), whose book, *Playing and Learning Outdoors,* explains how appropriate outdoor space needs to provide flexibility; a place where children can see the impact of their own efforts and engender a sense of curiosity and fascination.

LET'S COOK! LEARNING THROUGH IMMERSION IN PLAY

Ruby, who we met earlier with her younger brother Jonah, loves spending time with Naomi and her husband Jez, who is a professional cook. Do watch this film clip (mentioned in Figure 14.3, accessible via the QR code), where we managed to capture the delight on Ruby's face as she realises her dream of learning to be a chef. Her family ensures that her disability never prevents her from trying new activities. It's only a very short clip but the humour and playful learning is delightful to see.

LET'S COOK! THEORY EXPLAINED

Now, do watch this short film clip (mentioned in Figure 14.4, accessible via the QR code), where Naomi comments on what she sees is happening in the earlier clip with Ruby, from a play therapist's point of view. Naomi briefly explains the important work of the theorists, Piajet and Vygotsky.

Figure 14.3 Naomi and Jez. See video "Let's cook!" via the QR code

Figure 14.4 Naomi. See video "Naomi explains the benefits of play and cooking" via the QR code

Best practice: play pedagogy

With the statutory rollout of the updated (2021) *Early Years Foundation Stage (EYFS)*, and the introduction of the *Early Years Foundation Stage Profile (EYFSP)*, questions are beginning to emerge around:

- The general impact on early literacy and numeracy levels
- Best practice for creating a holistic curriculum
- Post-pandemic priorities for mitigating the impact on children's development
- Strategies for supporting mental health for both children and staff
- Strategies for responding to the impact of adverse childhood experiences
- Best practice play-based learning

Naomi says:

In my everyday practice, I use a variety of pedagogical approaches when providing for children's play activities. I think it is important to be sensitive to their needs and respond in a way that respects their individuality and personal interests – not treating a class as one homogeneous group. Children learn so much more efficiently when they are enthused and engaged – when the topic sparks their imagination and creativity, they actively want to participate. I am amazed at children's thirst for knowledge, their curiosity, and their drive to discover and try out new things for themselves.

BRAIN AND BODY SENSORY DEVELOPMENT POINTERS

Now we turn to examine child development more generally.

From around four years to around five years

General brain growth

According to Brown and Jernigan (2012:8), " … by age 4, the greatest changes in area are occurring within higher order cortical regions such as the prefrontal cortex and temporal association areas."

General social and emotional development

Around this age, there is quite a turning point in the young child's understanding of how their own actions may affect other people. She may even try to comfort another child when she realises she has upset them. At this stage, she wants to understand what is acceptable behaviour in her own culture. So, greater sensitivity and compassion towards others can be observed and the seeds of understanding of how to cooperate with others – particularly during play. However, playing alone will continue and often involves elaborate imaginative play. She can be strongly self-willed as the desire to be independent increases but she will still enjoy demonstrating a true sense of humour.

General physical development

Her physical abilities at this stage are impressive and she loves to show adults what she can do. She climbs the stairs with confidence and can run well: starting, stopping, and turning corners with control and a good sense of balance. She can stand or run on tiptoe and ride a tricycle, turning corners and climbing over large apparatus. Her ability to kick, throw, catch, and bounce a ball is something she often enjoys practising. She can bend now instead of squatting to pick up objects and can hold a pencil in a similar way to an adult. Around this stage, she will be showing increased fine motor skill development which allows the further refinement of hand–eye coordination. She may start to form some letters and her drawings will be more recognisable, for example, she will draw fingers on hands, and she may even discuss what she is about to draw or paint.

General communication and language development

A child around this age is full of questions! She will constantly ask: Why? When? How? Can I have? Can I go? She can also talk about future activities and loves to joke. She will appreciate the humour of absurdities and sentences like "A cow goes quack" will make her laugh out loud. Her vocabulary will be expanding, and she will explore the meanings and sounds of new words. She might really enjoy making up words. Interestingly (and rather cleverly!), she will try to make grammatically irregular words fit grammatical rules, for example, "I goed" instead of "I went." She will start using words such as "in," "on," and "under" but might find it difficult to pro-nounce sounds such as "r," "th," and "str" (in straw) or "scr" (in scrap) and "sp" (in crisps).

General cognitive and symbolic development

Another leap of development occurs around this age in the ability to solve simple problems, such as where to look for a lost toy. She can also provide explanations, such as why the plate is empty because she ate all of her food. She might enjoy repeating songs and nursery rhymes. When interested and cap-tivated, she can maintain attention and concentration and sits quietly during age-appropriate activities. Around this age, the young child will start to listen with purpose and with intention. She shows greater interest in the text when looking at picture books. Play can be quite detailed and planned – for example, giving prior consideration of where they might place play objects into a scene. Although she may still confuse fact and fiction, children around this age really enjoy experimenting with objects from everyday life. She can say numbers up to ten and beyond but the actual understanding of a number and what it really means may be less. Usually, she can match primary colours during a game.

FIVE-YEAR PLUS

Overall development trajectory: Increasingly, a child over the age of five will engage in elaborate play and will try hard to conform to rules and expectations in games. She will begin to show a preference for what she wants to do during play time and who she plays with. The ability to be even more imaginative in her play means that with very little formal playthings to hand, she will improvise and see new possibilities in any given play object. Egocentricity is now declining as she is learning to separate self from non-self and this gives way to a greater appreciation of how others might feel in a given situation. In terms of brain development, according to Kuzawa et al. (2014), the child's brain at around the age of five years is demanding almost twice as much energy to support its development compared to an adult's brain.

PLAY AND PEDAGOGY

Drawing again on the films in this chapter with Levi and the value of outdoor play, let's turn now to consider how theory can further underpin our understanding.

Playing outside

Outdoor play has been much debated with most researchers agreeing that children simply must spend more time outside. Many researchers, such as Burdette and Whitaker (2005), believe that children experience greater opportunities to develop their problem-solving skills and increase their creativity when outside. Of course, the most debated aspect concerns fears about children's safety when playing outside unsupervised (Clements, 2004). It is well established that the socio-cultural context will inevitably impact on play experiences. It is also widely believed (Gray, 2011) that outdoor play is on the decline in the West (UK, Europe, and America).

Factors that appear to impact play outdoors are:

- Reduction of appropriate outdoor play spaces
- Increase in traffic
- Lack of green space
- Less available time for adults to take their children outdoors

Figure 14.5 The outdoor space offers children the freedom to take risks and explore the limitations of their bodies

- More structured activities replacing outdoor playtime
- Attraction of indoor digital devices, gaming, and television

The outdoor space frequently offers young children a sense of empowerment and freedom not always experienced in indoor spaces. It tends to be unstructured and encourages creativity. Interestingly, once unstructured playtime at school has been introduced, several studies show that a child's ability to focus and concentrate on more formal learning is enhanced (Pelligrini & Holmes, 2006).

PLAY IT FORWARD

Building on the valuable play research explored above, we can consider a variety of suitable experiences (some of which we have already witnessed in the films).

Practical play-based sensory activities

Name	Description	Age range	Resources	Activity length	Possible brain and body benefit	Safety notes
Bowling	Challenge the child to turn plastic bottles for recycling into a bowling game. How many can they knock over?	4–6 years	Use bottles (ready to be recycled) filled with water. Place short ribbons around the bottlenecks (bottles can be decorated too by covering them with paper that can be coloured in) A ball	20–30 minutes	This activity can help with cultivating creativity, fostering fine motor control (as they decorate the bottles) and help with general understanding of the concept of numbers	Under general constant supervision
Send a letter and picture	Encourage her to make a card (using colouring pencils), put it in an envelope addressed to a friend with a stamp, and visit the postbox together	3–6 years	Stamp, envelope, paper, pencil, and colouring crayons	20–30 minutes	Children gradually understand that printed text has meaning This activity also provides the young child with the opportunity to become a skilled mark-maker	Take care crossing roads together
Indoors treasure hunt	Draw a very basic map of the room or house and show the child which items are going to be hidden there (pictures of the items can be shown as photos on the cards). Do try to use natural objects. Set a timer – can she find all the items in time?	4–6 years	Large pieces of card showing familiar items, such as natural objects to be hidden	20–30 minutes	This fun activity using a basic map can help to develop a sense of orientation, and a timer can help towards understanding time limits. This activity also promotes the development of observational skills Natural open-ended resources encourage an eco-friendly approach in the early years, where adults can also begin to discuss with children how to minimise waste or recycle objects	Under general constant supervision

Name	Description	Age range	Resources	Activity length	Possible brain and body benefit	Safety notes
Your own TV show	Talk to children about their favourite TV shows and encourage them to make up a script – you could write it down for them. They could make their own puppets for the show or use cuddly toys to feature in it. A large box acts as a TV screen	4–6 years	Puppets Large cardboard box cut with large opening to act as a TV "screen" A piece of paper to record their "script"	20–30 minutes	Through imaginative play, children learn to consider others' perspectives, transfer knowledge from one situation to another, develop a plan and act on it, and listen to thoughts and ideas	Under general constant supervision
My minibeast book	Gardens and outdoor spaces are full of minibeasts – try searching together and taking photos of any you find, then print out and make into a book	3–6 years	Camera, printer and card	15–40 minutes	This type of activity rewards children for being calm and patient when attempting to discover something interesting	Under general constant supervision

POINTERS FOR DIGGING DEEPER

Media literacy

Ofcom defines media literacy as "the ability to access, understand and create communications in a variety of contexts" (2006:2). The use of play and digital media is a highly contested area, yet most researchers now agree that children start to develop media literacy from early infancy, developing "a wide range of skills, knowledge and understanding of this world from birth" (Marsh et al., 2005:5). Both Buckingham (2007) and Marsh et al. (2005) agree that children will develop media literacy skills even if they are not in receipt of formal media education at school.

The brain and symbols

"The screen is now the dominant site of texts; it is the site which shapes the imagination of the current generation around communication …. This does not mean that writing cannot appear on screen, but when it does, it will be appearing there subordinated to the logic of the visual" (Kress, 2003:166).

The world is dominated by symbols which communicate a variety of meanings, and the young brain is working hard to decipher this constant communication. Symbols may include numbers, words, pictures, and signs. Essentially the demands on the brain to work out these meanings is a creative act in itself and deeply impressive.

Young children are encountering texts, images, video motion, and audio, with new assumptions about its organisation and hierarchy. New literacies, which encompass words and symbols, confront the "reader" with the need to analyse multiple representations. This new language is multi-modal and multi-layered.

Figure 14.6 Lily loves stories. Listening to stories and interpreting the pictures is an astounding feat for the developing brain

DISCUSSION STARTERS

Read this following paragraph and discuss any observations you have made of young children watching television:

Dr Dimitri Christakis is the director of the *Center for Child Health, Behavior and Development*. He and his team of researchers have made several important findings. For example, his work highlighted that early TV exposure, particularly to fast-paced shows, can lead to attentional challenges for children later in life (Christakis et al., 2004). There is a mounting need to research exactly *how* children are engaging with different media devices and moving between platforms; the drivers; what skills they are gaining from these new activities; what the benefits might be; how students, practitioners, and parents can best support these new activities and ultimately provide practical guidelines, and most importantly safeguard children against the challenges described by Dr Christakis.

REFLECTION POINTS

- The film clips of Leyla, Levi, and Ruby demonstrate that play can be fully immersive and fulfilling.
- Simple outdoor play offers children a place where they can be curious and explore.
- Unstructured play can enhance concentration skills.
- There is mounting concern about children's safety online.

15 "Hola" – Let's play! A case study

> **This chapter will introduce you to:**
> - A real nursery and will demonstrate how play can have a lasting positive impact on the lives of young children
> - The Reggio Emilia approach
> - The enduring and impactful work of Froebel
> - The value of outdoor sensory-based play

THE BRAIN LOVES TO PLAY

Do watch this film clip (mentioned in Figure 15.1, accessible via the QR code), where Lourdes, the manager of the nursery, speaks of her play pedagogy and why she also believes that the young developing brain loves to play. Alma and Anvilona, who assist her in the nursery, also share her values and vision for the nursery.

EXPERIMENTING IN PLAY: THE WATER HOSE

In this compelling film clip (mentioned in Figure 15.4, accessible via the QR code), Dexter who is two and a half years old is experimenting with watering the plants. Lourdes, who was also present at the time, provides an additional running commentary which discusses his behaviour and how the activity relates to good early years practice. She proposes ways in which the play could be extended.

DOI: 10.4324/9781003309758-16

Figure 15.1 Lourdes in her nursery. See video "Lourdes' nursery" via the QR code

Figure 15.2 Anvilona Ajazi is deputy manager and their safeguarding officer

Figure 15.3 Alma Sykaj is the nursery nurse at the nursery

Figure 15.4 Dexter. See video "The water hose" via the QR code

Figure 15.5 Dexter is fascinated by the water emerging from the hose

CHILDREN'S AGENCY – THEIR INTERESTS ARE THE STARTING POINT: THE BOX OF BEES

Do take time to watch this film clip (mentioned in Figure 15.6, accessible via the QR code), where an opportunity arises for Lily to consider numbers and follow her individual interest in the colour yellow.

THE BOX OF BEES EXPLAINED

Why not follow up your viewing of the last film clip about the box of bees with this next clip (mentioned in Figure 15.7, accessible via the QR code), where Lourdes explains the box of bees activity and how she considers the child's fascination with an enveloping schema (see page 219).

Figure 15.6 Lily. See video "The box of bees" via the QR code

Figure 15.7 Lourdes. See video "Lourdes explains the box of bees" via the QR code

Figure 15.8 Lily and the dog investigate the box of bees

A FROG APPEARS: IMMERSION IN PLAY

Why not immerse yourself in this delightful film (mentioned in Figure 15.9, accessible via the QR code), where five children discuss the sudden appearance of a frog in a padding pool. They each raise several theories about the event and their conversations are treated with respect. The excitement of the frog's discovery demonstrates playful exploration that compels children to immerse themselves in the moment within a bubble of timelessness (Csikszentmihalyi, 1991).

Figure 15.9 The children in the nursery. See video "A frog appears" via the QR code

THE ANTS AND THE MAGNIFYING GLASS: IMMERSION IN PLAY

The ants arrive in this deeply interesting film clip (mentioned in Figure 15.10, accessible via the QR code), which provides the children with an opportunity to talk about size comparisons. The children eagerly contribute to the discussions. A magnifying glass helps the process.

THE ANTS AND THE MAGNIFYING GLASS EXPLAINED

Lourdes now explains how adults' plans for play often need to be changed or adapted according to the needs and interests of the child. Do watch this film clip (mentioned in Figure 15.11,

Figure 15.10 Dexter. See video "The ants and the magnifying glass" via the QR code

Figure 15.11 Lourdes. See video "Lourdes explains how the ants and the magnifying glass activity emerged" via the QR code

accessible via the QR code), as she considers the importance of acknowledging the interests of the child.

THE ELEPHANT RHYME AND IMMERSION IN PLAY

Do watch this film clip (mentioned in Figure 15.12, accessible via the QR code), where the children are playing and enjoying a rhyme together. The sheer anticipation of their favourite part is clear to see!

CASE STUDY

"Hola!" says Lourdes, who is the manager at White Rose nursery and originally from Venezuela (we have met Lourdes and some of the children in her nursery in earlier chapters). Several of the children are bilingual.

As an early years teacher and lecturer in the importance of early years intervention at a local university, she is passionate about the therapeutic value of play. She is also undertaking an MSc

Figure 15.12 Matilda and her friends enjoy rhymes together. See video "Elephant rhyme" via the QR code

Figure 15.13 Rhymes and songs offer significant gains in language development

in educational psychology, and her play provision reflects her understanding of how play through the senses brings joy to the developing brain!

Her nursery has a very large garden, where the children spend most of their day. It is packed with natural resources for the children to explore. Lourdes is also an advocate of the Reggio Emilia approach. She says,

> I became fascinated by an approach to learning in the early years that gives rights to the learner. In this approach, children are active constructors of knowledge. I like the way in which the adult role is one of collaborator, in other words, co-learner alongside the child. It feels such a respectful way to teach.

She also finds this approach resonates with her love of nature.

Figure 15.14 Malleable materials bring joy to the brain that loves to create and imagine! Dexter enjoys the feel of the dough in his hands

Figure 15.15 The natural world is a rich source of play and learning

Best practice: schemas

In the films above, it is evident that some of the children are exploring particular schemas (see Chapter 11 for further information about schemas). Here are some suggestions for simple activities to further support a child's schema(s):

Transporting: Shopping baskets, diggers, and trucks to transport dirt/sand, purses/bags to fill and carry, putting shopping away, and moving objects from container to another

Enveloping: Hiding toys in sand, wrapping presents, sock puppets, dressing up, baking – pies and pastries

Enclosure/Containing: Cardboard box house, colouring inside a box, tents/forts made from sheets, coin drop box, and a playdough home for animals

Trajectory: Paper planes, yoyos, ball throwing games, frisbee, kites

Rotation: Rolling playdough, painting with rollers, mixing and stirring ingredients, hula hoops, bangles, and bracelets

Connection: Paper chains, spider webs with string, jigsaw puzzles, containers with lids, and putting pen caps/lids on and off

Positioning: Sorting activities, tracing shapes and matching them, balancing objects, and 3D art (buttons, beads, shell, etc.)

Transforming: Cooking (making dough), food colouring activities, playdough, face painting, and colour mixing

Figure 15.16 Playing in the mud kitchen delights the developing brain! Hana is engrossed in her play

PLAY AND PEDAGOGY

Sensory play is the golden thread that runs through all that is on offer in this nursery. Lourdes stresses the importance of promoting overall well-being for the families that attend her nursery. Lourdes comments that last week one child said, "I feel so warm and snug in the den." And recently another child said, "This is my safe place," as he tucked himself into the fairy den.

In the garden, there is a mud kitchen, a den, a bug hotel, and other creative facilities. Lourdes ensures that the children have access to sand and water play, planting, and other gardening activities, also building fairy gardens …. She said, "The children spend a lot of time running up and down the garden and spinning round in circles." Parents comment on the experience, for example, "This nursery is such a nurturing experience that I can't recommend the place enough." And another said, "I love how much time the children spend outside in the huge garden … developing imagination and creativity."

Figure 15.17 Matilda (left) and Emma (right) enjoy spending time outdoors in the nursery

Figure 15.18 The outdoor environment offers children an opportunity to think more about wildlife. Dexter is curious about the bug hotel

The work of Froebel

Froebel started the kindergarten movement. It is interesting to note just how Froebelian theories are still at the centre of good practice in early years care and education. Froebel was a solid believer in creative play and interestingly saw that their best learning takes place when children are immersed and engrossed in imaginative play. He believed that this kind of deep play evoked a kind of deep-level thinking. Froebel's theories embraced the outdoor space which he saw promoted freedom of movement and encouraged sensory exploration. Creative activities such as arts and crafts, music, and books were top of his list of activities that were most beneficial for children.

Figure 15.19 The living world offers all-round benefits to the development of the body and brain

Inclusive practice

Conscious of the need to avoid gender stereotyping during play in her nursery, Lourdes says,

Over the years of experience in teaching early years, I've noticed just how early children begin to learn about gender roles. They tend to pick up messages so quickly about what is expected from a girl or boy. That is really unhelpful. It is important to me that children absorb the message that I allow enough resources for them to play and explore freely without limitations. There must be no assumptions about what they might like to play with based on their gender.

Lourdes believes that, with support, young children can develop positive and generous attitudes towards themselves and others. This is achieved through careful choice of vocabulary and the way in which staff behave towards each other and the children. She comments, "I am sad that even today so many families face prejudice and discrimination. It may be a slow process but I believe that through early education we can make better progress that will have a lasting impact."

Figure 15.20 Kindness and generosity of thought is key to supporting young children

PLAY IT FORWARD

Practical play-based sensory activities

The following three activities are ones that have been tried and tested at the White Rose nursery.

Name	Description	Age range	Resources	Activity length	Possible brain and body benefit	Safety notes
Keeping an eye on the natural world	Provide children with a detective's cap, a large notebook and crayons … then set off to explore the natural world. What can they find? Encourage them to look closely under pebbles	2–3 years	Magnifying glasses (child-safe)	10–30 minutes	Children can be co-constructors of knowledge – as it places them in the driving seat. Young children are subject to the routine and rules and regulations of life – in play they can feel just a little "power" which can help them feel more in control!	Ensure magnifying glasses are safe for children
Mud, glorious mud	A mud kitchen need not be elaborate – just use simple old pans and watering cans, and perhaps a bowl. Children are capable of imagining the rest of the kitchen! Of course, the more safe bits and pieces, such as wooden spoons, old cake tins, and bowls you can offer – the more there is to experiment with. Plenty of mud is also needed	2–4 years	Mud Utensils Watering cans Pans Bowls	10–30 minutes	Simple activities like this can go a long way in stimulating the imagination and the act of dreaming and pretence is good for the brain. Role-play is deeply interesting to young children and they revel in the opportunity to take charge in their own play scenarios "What if" questions can be the starting point for rich small world play and role-play which transport children into imaginary worlds	Take care with sharp or rusty materials Constant supervision is always required

(Continued)

225

Name	Description	Age range	Resources	Activity length	Possible brain and body benefit	Safety notes
Repetitive rhymes	Rhymes with young children seem to hold even more fascination when they have an item in their hands – it adds to the fun and involvement. Try rhymes, such as the elephant song in the film above. Or, try making up rhymes using everyday objects and toys	4–5 years	An item that each child can hold, such as an elephant to accompany a familiar rhyme or song	5–10 minutes	Repetitive rhymes brim over with opportunities to laugh together in anticipation of "the big moment" within children's favourite rhymes. Play and imagination collide and erupt into times of humour. Adults and children can share in those delightful times: "moments of meeting," joint attention, and fun	

POINTERS FOR DIGGING DEEPER

Reggio Emilia

Reggio Emilia is in Northern Italy. It has become well known and respected for its effective and innovative early years system.

> *The Reggio Emilia Approach to educating young children is strongly influenced by a unique image of the child and deeply embedded within the surrounding culture. It is not a model nor recipe with a set of guidelines and procedures to be followed, therefore, one cannot and should not attempt to simply import it to another location. Rather, it must be carefully uncovered and redefined according to one's own culture in order to successfully affect practice elsewhere.*

> (Hewett, 2001:99)

The Reggio Emilia approach is focussed on the early years and primary education and is both an educational philosophy and play pedagogy. It is child-centred and recognises that children are capable of constructing their own learning. It also recognises the importance of relationships within the child's own community as rich sources of support and learning. The approach is also empowering in its recognition that children are natural communicators.

DISCUSSION STARTERS

Reflect on the films taken in the nursery and the way in which the children are trusted to lead the play. Now, imagine that you have been given the responsibility of choosing a sensory-based activity for one of the children in the films. Consider the ways in which the child might be encouraged to be a co-constructor of knowledge.

REFLECTION POINTS

- The film clips all demonstrate the children's developing sense of agency over their play choices.
- The Reggio Emilia approach is an empowering one – with the child taking centre stage and capable of building their own learning.
- Froebel's work was pioneering and his legacy lives on today in good early years practice in care and education.
- Outdoor play offers rich opportunities for sensory-based play. It evokes the full range of senses and delights the developing brain.
- Children enjoy the role of being a co-constructor of knowledge – as it places them in the driving seat. In play, they can feel just a little "power" which can help them feel more in control when life becomes frustrating and confusing.

16 What's so urgent about play for children? And how does play benefit adults?

This chapter will introduce you to:

* The urgency of play for young children and … you – the reader. With all the benefits of play expounded in this book, surely there must be a little time to explore why play might be important to adults and how we can make sure it continues throughout life? But first, returning to children …

CREATIVE WELL-BEING IS GOLD DUST TO THE BRAIN

Please do take time to watch this film clip (mentioned in Figure 16.1, accessible via the QR code), where I make a plea for the untold riches of play and creative well-being to be recognised for the gold it can offer children and adults.

Play and pedagogy

Creative well-being

In 2006, alongside a medical doctor, Dr Sanjay Chaudhuri, I was asked to research the possible impact of a more creative curriculum on six- and seven-year-olds in two disadvantaged areas. The research was commissioned by Creative Partnerships and published in 2008. It told the story of creative well-being through an extraordinary set of events that occurred in two pioneering schools during the summer and autumn terms of 2006. The schools in Basildon were supported

DOI: 10.4324/9781003309758-17

Figure 16.1 Jacqueline. See video "Creative well-being is gold dust" via the QR code

by Creative Partnerships, who commissioned two artists to work directly with children in the classroom: they encouraged a creative approach to their work in line with Creative Partnerships' policy of "exciting minds." Meanwhile, as researchers, Dr Chaudhuri and I were to examine the creative process itself, to identify its key stages and see how they come together in a single inspirational moment. Central to the work were individual breakthroughs and setbacks, play, humour, and curiosity of the children and teachers at the two schools, and the fascinating relationships they developed with the artists over the two terms.

Equally central to the story was the neurological perspective, for when children of all ages engage in creative pursuits, their brains are signal processing at a higher level. They are literally seeing, sensing, hearing, and feeling more of the world. Scientists agree that long-term health and well-being rests upon a feeling of creative autonomy and expression. Each of us needs to know that we are creating something that "belongs to us," and that our creative expressions are valued. We need not produce the perfect painting, musical composition, or sculpture but our creative

Figure 16.2 Children and adults have a biological drive to be imaginative and creative as Lily and Sienna demonstrate in their immersion in this rich play activity. The expansiveness of play is the generous space for a child to be curious and explore. Play can make a world of difference to our well-being

expressions should mean something personal to us and, from a medical perspective, engage our minds and bodies.

Dr Chaudhuri pointed out that there are two opposing biological forces within human beings: firstly, we have a need for predictability. This causes us to be naturally conservative. In order to maintain homeostasis, we tend not to take risks or make changes; we try to keep things as they are. Secondly, we have a need for change, growth, and unpredictability. This need adds another design feature, which allows us to meet life's challenges by questioning and changing our thought processes. This very process can lead to the act of creativity.

Creative education strives to achieve a better balance between the two physiological mechanisms. Traditional education is far more in favour of fixed, controlled mechanisms at the expense of the dynamic factors that nurture creativity. And yet, the seemingly chaotic brain processes that generate creative thought are transposed onto the body in the calmest fashion. When children are deeply engaged in the creative moment, their bodies appear to be highly controlled. Their attention is wholly directed towards the activity in hand.

Persistence

Persistence is a measure of how long a child will be lost in concentration during the creative activity. Children who are really involved do not let go of the activity easily. They want to prolong the satisfaction, flavour, and intensity it gives them and will make considerable efforts to do so. They will not be easily distracted. The more "involved" the activity, the more prolonged their attention. However, persistence is also dependent on the age and the development of the child.

Precision

Involved children show special care for their work and are attentive to detail. This corresponds to very finely controlled muscle movement and hand–eye control. Non-involved children gloss over such detail, as it is not so important to them (Laevers, 1994).

Our work highlighted the biological, educational, and social dimensions of creativity and suggested that creativity in all its forms should underpin the status of schools as centres of health and well-being as well as centres for learning. We drew critical attention to the educational, social, and emotional benefits of a creative approach to the curriculum. It was the result of a sincere exploration into creativity and its effects on children. It was also the product of a rare collaboration that searched into the art and science of creativity in the classroom. Most importantly, our research questioned the way education is experienced from a medical perspective. Like any other medical ailment, the emotional problems suffered by children in education will only get worse unless we act to change the system.

Play we must!

Mulligan et al. (2012) assert that play is a natural resource for children to develop resilience. The authors believe that through playing with their children, parents have time to bond with them and begin to see the world from their child's perspective. The researchers also express deep concern for children living in poverty and how that may impede their right to playtime and subsequent healthy social-emotional development. They are adamant that it is now critical for all those working with young families to truly understand that play has benefits that can be reaped throughout life.

Fresh and inspired approaches to play and learning

Despite wide-ranging research that highlights the all-round benefits of a more playful approach to learning (Sproule, Walsh, & McGuinness, 2019), it seems that the debate continues to rage. The narrative of play as a description of a process that is simply the opposite of work is baffling

Figure 16.3 Valuing play and its inherent developmental benefits can redefine what we mean by "education"!

in the light of its extensive contribution to human development. As Sturrock, Else, and Russell (2004) point out, the important place of play appears to need defending by each new generation. Professor Pat Preedy has become increasingly concerned about the pedagogical divide between reception and year one and points out that the early years foundation stage does not cover birth to seven years in an adequate manner. In the notable book: *Early Childhood Education Redefined: Reflections and Recommendations on the Impact of Start Right* (Preedy, Sanderson, & Ball, 2018), the authors draw attention to three areas of weakness in the provision of education for young children over the last 20 years: support of parents, education, and pedagogy from birth to seven years.

Small steps

With emerging research into brain growth, we can harvest some of this new data to help us all take baby steps forward with a new paradigm that is more sensitive to a brain and body development-based approach to play and its value to all-round development. As Conkbayir (2021:302) points out, there seems to be quite a journey to travel to achieve an interdisciplinary relationship that might make best use of translating findings from neuroscience research into useful practice for practitioners ... "continual refining and collaboration across neuroscientists and practitioners will need to be carefully coordinated to ensure that the application of neuroscience leads to theories that can be applied to early childhood practice."

Most practitioners and those researching in the field agree that the way ahead might include repeatedly exemplifying good playful practice (some even point to the need for video evidence to embed a deeper understanding). Hopefully this book goes some way to addressing the solution and silencing some of the tired debates and inspiring all adults to embrace a more playful approach to learning and life for the sake of all our children.

Figure 16.4 The brain lights up with joy at the thought of learning through play

Pressure cooker children

Recipe: Place one fully operational, active, and energetic young child into a cooking pot of compressed and over-refined experiences, deprive the child of sustained human contact, replace the lid and so eliminate the chance of exposure and engagement with a helpful community, and shake vigorously. *Result*: One depressed and angry youth.

Many educators agree that children today are under an incredible amount of pressure: peer pressure, media, and consumer pressure, and more importantly there is an invisible reaction to the stress that their parents experience. A familiar and repeated cry from parents is: "When my child is stressed – I'm stressed." A cyclical pattern of pressure. They can explode, get difficult, depressed, awkward, violent, disrespectful, or just withdraw, shut down, and be less communicative.

Short-term stress for a child isn't serious – mostly they bounce back very quickly. It's when stress becomes chronic and unremitting that over-pressured children can start to show medical symptoms. There has been a dramatic increase in lifestyle-related illness among children and there is growing concern in the rise of stress-related cases among children attending GP surgeries. Childhood stress is associated with an increase in headaches, asthma, eczema, anxiety, depression, as well as gastrointestinal problems, such as stomach aches and irritable bowel syndrome (IBS).

Recipe: Take one fully operational, active and energetic young child and give them five portions of play a day; look them in the eyes and connect with them at least three times a day; listen to what the child has to say and hug vigorously. *Result*: One well-adjusted youth on the way to being a calm and happy parent one day.

The four costs of severe pressure and stress on children today:

1 Certain pressure undermines children's ability to concentrate and learn, thus jeopardising their education
2 Stressed children are more at risk of becoming stressed adults
3 Elevated cortisol levels may mean that brain growth is slowed down, learning is impaired, and immune systems are weakened
4 Severe and prolonged stress causes a range of illnesses, from asthma to IBS

The true value of play

Previous chapters have outlined how these effects of play go far beyond the notion of simply keeping children (and adults) occupied. In fact, emerging educational and health-based research is beginning to reveal that play is nature's well-kept secret, a high-performance learning tool.

In earlier chapters, we explored neuroplasticity, which simply means that with support, the brain can change and develop throughout life. The way to combat the brain aging process is to improve neurogenesis (the birth of new neurons). Although neurogenesis occurs more in the

Figure 16.5 Janos and his dad enjoy laughing and this creates close connection

early years, there is now no doubt that this can still happen for adults. So, how do we as adults protect our brains? We need to actively seek out experiences that light up the brain, such as meeting new people. Young children are not the only ones in need of social interaction in order to thrive, adults also need this in later life. So, visit different places – get plenty of sleep … and laugh! Then, we are more likely to encourage neurogenesis. It seems from research that there is a compelling argument for infusing our lives/brains with humour. We now know that laughter is modulated by social context (basically the origins of humour lie in social connection according to Gervais & Wilson, 2005). Simply being with others who are laughing is contagious; we "catch" laughter. And, it is good for our well-being.

For the sake of brevity, here are perhaps six of the most important benefits of play but this time they need to be read from a different perspective – another lens … just how it might help grownups too?

1 Builds self-esteem and confidence
2 Accelerates learning and academic performance
3 Helps navigate the world's challenges
4 Creates better health
5 Stimulates brain development
6 Develops social skills

With these benefits in mind, the following top ten tips provide ways in which we can all reap some of those outstanding benefits of play – even as we mature:

1 Whenever possible, take time outdoors where your eyes can feast upon the colour green. This calms the nervous system.
2 Be a play companion to children in your care if it is in their best interest – I'm not suggesting *you* take over their play! If given their permission, immerse yourself in their world – let imagination do its greatest work on your brain too.
3 If you are physically able, run don't stroll – it's energising. (Remember children have much to teach us – they will never walk if given the chance to run instead!)
4 Soothe your mind by taking notice of your breathing and indulge in something calming such as picking up colouring pencils and simply enjoy a colouring-in book.
5 Be curious. Find your "happy place." Remember what it feels like to stop and stare, pause, and reflect.
6 Get creative. Find a hobby that delights you, although it may take a while to find that special project that feels "yours." Do try out new activities, perhaps using clay or paint.
7 Do something a little different every day – even walking backwards (safely when you can!) shakes the cobwebs off from the brain!
8 Give your brain a workout. Challenge it with something fun to solve.

Figure 16.6 My happy place!

9 Simply play in a way that sends *you* into the zone – a timeless place where everything stands still and allows you time to breathe.
10 Laugh when given the chance – a wholehearted belly laugh is a great workout.

Finally, here's a picture of my happy place. I am fortunate that it is only a few minutes away and I can walk there every day … well, actually … I often skip with absolute abandon!

DISCUSSION STARTERS

- Reflecting on the numerous film clips in this book of children playing, how important do you think it is for children to be free to play in the way that suits their needs? In your opinion, how vital is sensitively planned sensory-based play to a child's all-round development?
- Reflecting on the film contributions from adults throughout this book, what do you see as a priority for research of children's play that has the potential to make a positive difference to the quality of play provision for young children?

Figure 16.7 We must continue to "hunt" for those playful moments that make all the difference to our lives

REFLECTION POINTS

- As all the films in this book have testified, play is one of the richest ingredients that builds brains right from the start of life.
- Laughter and creativity seem to provide the glue for making learning "stick" in the mind!
- We all need to continue to play throughout our lives to keep the brain happily firing away and keep us all connecting socially and glowing with health.

17 Helpful websites

BABY CENTRE UK

This UK site works to support parents with babies and young children:

https://www.babycentre.co.uk/

BRAIN AND SPINE FOUNDATION

This site provides information about the anatomy and functions of the brain:

https://www.brainandspine.org.uk/information-and-support/anatomy-of-the-brain-and-spine/

BRAZELTON CENTRE UK

The Brazelton Centre UK is a national charity dedicated to supporting healthy parent–baby relationships through promoting an understanding of newborn babies' communication:

https://www.brazelton.co.uk/

BRIGHT START FOUNDATION

Bright Start Foundation is a non-profit organisation that works towards improving the quality of early childhood education and care as well as supporting and engaging parents as active partners:

https://brightstartfoundation.org/

DOI: 10.4324/9781003309758-18

EARLY EDUCATION

Early Education is a charity and membership organisation for individuals and organisations working in early childhood education across the United Kingdom:

https://early-education.org.uk/

EARLY YEARS MATTERS

This site is dedicated to providing high-quality training, information, and services on issues that affect young children's learning and development:

https://www.earlyyearsmatters.co.uk/

FAMILY LIVES

Family Lives provides targeted early intervention and crisis support to families:

https://www.familylives.org.uk/

FULLSPEKTRUM LTD.

FullSpektrum Ltd. (FS) is a London-based technology company, helping organisations to take a human-centred approach to information management, catering towards the "full-spectrum" of Education, Health and Social Care (EHC) services and alternative provisions:

https://fullspektrum.co.uk/

FROEBEL TRUST

Their aim is to ensure that the Froebelian framework of principled education and care is recognised, understood, valued and practised across the early childhood sector for the benefit of young children in the United Kingdom and internationally:

https://www.froebel.org.uk/

MUSIC COGNITION COMMUNICATION LAB (MUSICARE)

At the MCC Lab, Dr Fabia Franco and her team study psychological processes linked with music. They are interested in how human behaviours, thoughts, emotions, motor, and physiological responses are related to music and vice-versa:

https://mcclabmdx.com

NATIONAL CHILDBIRTH TRUST

The National Childbirth Trust is a national charity for pregnancy, birth and early parenthood:

https://www.nct.org.uk/

NATIONAL CHILDREN'S BUREAU

Working with children, and for children, NCB strives to reduce the devastating impact of inequalities:

https://www.ncb.org.uk/

NATIONAL SOCIETY FOR THE PREVENTION OF CRUELTY TO CHILDREN (NSPCC)

The National Society for the Prevention of Cruelty to Children provides information about how childhood experiences affect brain development:

https://learning.nspcc.org.uk/child-health-development/childhood-trauma-brain-development #heading-top

PLAY ENGLAND

Play England's vision is for England to be a country where everybody can fully enjoy their right to play throughout their childhood and teenage years, as set out in the UN Convention on the Rights of the Child Article 31 and the Charter for Children's Play:

https://www.playengland.org.uk/

PLAY PARTNERS PROJECT

The Play Partners Project has been extended across a wider audience through workshops organised by schools within the UAE. It is now available at no charge to schools and settings (via www.playpartnersproject.com). It also forms part of a Cache-endorsed online course through Laser Learning for early years educators written by Professor Pat Preedy and Rosie Hamilton-McGinty (A Winning Attitude Parent Workshops):

www.awaparentworkshops.com

PLAY SCOTLAND

Play Scotland is the lead organisation for the development and promotion of children and young people's play in Scotland:

https://www.playscotland.org/

RIGHT TO PLAY

Right to Play is a global organisation that protects, educates, and empowers children to rise above adversity using play:

https://www.righttoplay.org.uk/en-uk/

WORLD AFRO DAY

World Afro Day is a global day of change, education, and celebration of Afro hair, culture, and identity:

www.worldafroday.com

Glossary of terms

Adverse childhood experiences (ACEs): Adverse childhood experiences are stressful and traumatic events which occur during childhood.

Attachment bond: A baby's emotional connection to their primary carer is described as the attachment bond.

Creative opportunities: Artists create opportunities designed to engage the children's brains to undergo changes in energy and information flow. These changes are characterised by observable phenomena known as creative signals.

Creative well-being: A term meaning a state of mind-body health, happiness, and fulfilment, characterised by numerous creative signals.

Creativity: There are numerous interpretations of the word creativity. Creative partnerships focus on the notion of "exciting minds." Creativity is not a skill bound within the arts, but a wider ability to question, make connections, and take an innovative and imaginative approach to problem solving.

Developmental trajectories: Developmental trajectories describe the progression of all-round development.

Early regulatory disorders: Early regulatory disorders is a term to describe babies who have challenges with regulating their behaviour, such as excessive crying, problems with sleeping, and problems with feeding.

Kinship carers: A kinship carer is a person who cares for the child of a relative or friend on a full-time basis, for example, aunts, uncles, siblings, grandparents, family friends, or neighbours.

Multidisciplinary care: Multidisciplinary care is an integrated approach to care and support. It is offered by professionals from two or more different specialisms from across health, social care, and community care services.

Neural connections: This term concerns the connections between cells in the brain which enable basic functions.

Neuroscience: The study of the brain and its structure and function. With new imaging technology, we are learning more about the creative brain.

Ofsted: Ofsted is the regulatory body for education and children's social care services.

Perinatal: The perinatal period is the time from pregnancy up until one year after a baby's birth.

Safeguarding: In this book, the term safeguarding means the safeguarding of babies and children and assumes the need to act to protect them from harm and promote their welfare.

Sensory pathways: Sensory pathways is a term that describes the neural connections which are responsible for the perception of sight, sound, smell, taste, and touch.

Special educational needs: These terms should be understood as outlined in the *Special educational needs and disability code of practice: 0 to 25 years*; a child of compulsory school age or a young person has a learning difficulty or disability if he or she:

- Has a significantly greater difficulty in learning than the majority of others of the same age
- Has a disability which prevents or hinders him or her from making use of facilities of a kind generally provided for others of the same age in mainstream schools or mainstream post-16 institutions.

Start for life period: This period refers to the 1,001 critical days between conception and the age of two.

References

Adam, E. K., & Gunnar, M. R., (2001). Relationship functioning and home and work demands predict individual differences in diurnal cortisol patterns in women. *Psychoneuroendocrinology*, *26*(2), 189–208.

Ainsworth, M. D. S., Bell, S. M., & Stayton, D. J., (1974). Infant–mother attachment and social development: Socialisation as a product of reciprocal responsiveness to signals. In M. P. M. Richards (Ed.), *The Integration of a Child into a Social World* (pp. 99–135). New York: Cambridge University Press.

Ainsworth, M. D. S., Blehar, M. C., Waters, E., & Wall, S., (1978). *Patterns of Attachment*. Hillsdale, NJ: Erlbaum.

Asmussen, K., Fischer, F., Drayton, E., & McBride, T., (2020). Adverse childhood experiences: What we know, what we don't know, and what should happen next. *Early Intervention Foundation*, *18*(3), 882–902.

Athey, C., (2007). *Extending Thought in Young Children* (2nd ed.). London: Paul Chapman Publishing Ltd.

Atzil, S., Hendler, T., & Feldman, R., (2014). The brain basis of social synchrony. *Social Cognitive and Affective Neuroscience*, *9*(8), 1193–1202. https://doi.org/10.1093/scan/nst105

Axline, V. M., (1989). *Play Therapy*. Edinburgh: Churchill Livingstone.

Bandura, A., (1986). *Social Foundations of Thought and Action: A Social Cognitive Theory*. Hoboken: Prentice-Hall, Inc.

Bellerose, J. S., Beauchamp, M. H., & Lassonde, M., (2011). New insights into neurocognition provided by brain mapping: Social cognition and theory of mind. In H. Duffau (Ed.), *Brain Mapping*. Vienna: Springer. https://doi.org/10.1007/978-3-7091-0723-2_14

Best Beginnings, Home-Start UK, (2020). Parent-Infant Foundation. *Babies in Lockdown: Listening to Parents to Build Back Better*. Available at: https://babiesinlockdown.info/about/ (Accessed 23 Aug 2022).

Bhana, D., & Mayeza, E., (2016). We don't play with gays, they're not real boys ... they can't fight: Hegemonic masculinity and (homophobic) violence in the primary years of schooling. *International Journal of Educational Development*, *51*, 36–42.

Blakemore, S. J., & Frith, U., (2005). *The Learning Brain: Lessons for Education*. Oxford: Blackwell.

Boutte, G. S., Lopez-Robertson, J., & Powers-Costello, E., (2011). Moving beyond colorblindness in early childhood classrooms. *Early Childhood Education Journal*, *39*(5), 335–342.

Bowlby, J., (1969). *Attachment and Loss, Volume 1, Attachment*. New York: Basic Books.

Bowlby, J., (1979). *The Making and Breaking of Affectional Bonds*. London: Routledge.

Braungart-Rieker, J. M., Garwood, M. M., Powers, B. P., & Wang, X., (2001). Parental sensitivity, infant affect, and affect regulation: Predictors of later attachment. *Child Development*, *72*(1), 252–270.

Brazelton, T. B., & Als, H., (1979). Four early stages in the development of mother-infant interaction. *The Psychoanalytic Study of the Child*, *34*(1), 349–369.

Broadhead, P., (2009). Conflict resolution and children's behaviour: Observing and understanding social and cooperative play in early years educational settings. *Early Years*, *29*(2), 105–118.

Broesch, T., & Bryant, G. A., (2018). Fathers' infant-directed speech in a small-scale society. *Child Development*, *89*(2), e29–e41.

Broesch, T. L., & Bryant, G. A., (2015). Prosody in infant-directed speech is similar across western and traditional cultures. *Journal of Cognition and Development*, *16*(1), 31–43.

Bronfenbrenner, U., (1988). Interacting systems in human development: Research paradigms: Present and future. In N. Bolger, A. Caspi, G. Downey, & M. Moorehouse (Eds.), *Persons in Context: Developmental Processes* (pp. 25–49). Cambridge: University Press.

Brown, S., Bekoff, M., & Myers, J., (1998). *Play as an Organizing Principle: Clinical Evidence and Personal Observations*. Cambridge: University Press.

Brown, T. T., & Jernigan, T. L., (2012). Brain development during the preschool years. *Neuropsychology Review*, *22*(4), 313–333. https://doi.org/10.1007/s11065-012-9214-1

Brown, S., & Vaughan, C., (2009). *Child Learning, Children's Play, Introduction to Play, Play Science*. London: Penguin Random House.

Bruce, T., (2011). *Learning Through Play* (2nd ed.). Abingdon: Hodder Education.

Bruner, J., (1983). The acquisition of pragmatic commitments. *The Transition from Prelinguistic to Linguistic Communication*, *1983*, 27–42.

Buchsbaum, D., Bridgers, S., Skolnick Weisberg, D., & Gopnik, A., (2012). The power of possibility: Causal learning, counterfactual reasoning, and pretend play. *Philosophical Transactions of the Royal Society B: Biological Sciences*, *367*(1599), 2202–2212. https://doi.org/10.1098/rstb.2012.0122

Buckingham, D., (2007). *Beyond Technology: Children Learning in the Age of Digital Culture*. Cambridge: Polity Press.

Burdette, H. L., & Whitaker, R. C., (2005). Resurrecting free play in young children: Looking beyond fitness and fatness to attention, affiliation, and affect. *Archives of Pediatrics and Adolescent Medicine*, *159*(1), 46–50.

Butterworth, G., & Grover, L., (1988). The origins of referential communication in human infancy. In L. Weiskrantz (Ed.), *Thought without Language* (pp. 5–24). Oxford: Clarendon Press/Oxford University Press.

Cadwell, L. B., (2003). *Bringing Learning to Life: The Reggio Approach to Early Childhood Education*. New York: Teachers College Press.

Chappell, P. F., & Sander, L. W., (1979). Mutual regulation of the neonatal–maternal interactive process: Context for the origins of communication. In M. Bullowa (Ed.), *Before Speech: The Beginning of Interpersonal Communication* (pp. 111–130). New York: Cambridge University Press.

Cherney, I. D., & Dempsey, J., (2010). Young children's classification, stereotyping and play behaviour for gender neutral and ambiguous toys. *Educational Psychology*, *30*(6), 651–669.

Children and Families Act, (2014) Children. [online] Available at: http://www.ccinform.co.uk/legislation/children-families-act-2014/#adoption (Accessed 7 Feb 2023).

Children's Commissioner, (2020). *Best Beginnings in the Early Years*. Available at: content/uploads/2020/07/cco-bestbeginnings-in-the-early-years.pdf (Accessed 23 Aug 2022).

Christakis, D. A., (2020). Pediatrics and COVID-19. *Journal of the American Medical Association*, *324*(12), 1147–1148.

Christakis, D. A., Zimmerman, F. J., DiGiuseppe, D. L., & McCarty, C. A., (2004). Early television exposure and subsequent attentional problems in children. *Pediatrics*, *113*(4), 708–713.

Churches, R., Dommentt, E., & Devonshire, I., (2017). *Neuroscience for Teachers Applying Research Evidence from Brain Science*. Carmarthen: Crown House Publishing.

Cicchetti, D., & Walker, E., (2001). Editorial: Stress and development: Biological and psychological conse-quences. *Development and Psychopathology*, *13*(3), 413–418. https://doi.org/10.1017/S095457940 1003017

Clements, R., (2004). An investigation of the status of outdoor play. *Contemporary Issues in Early Childhood*, 5(1), 68–80.

Conkbayir, M., (2021). *Early Childhood and Neuroscience Theory, Research and Implications for Practice.* London: Bloomsbury.

Cozolino, L., (2014). *The Neuroscience of Human Relationships: Attachment and the Developing Social Brain (Norton Series on Interpersonal Neurobiology)*. WW Norton & Company.

Cremin, T., Burnard, P., & Craft, A., (2006). Pedagogy and possibility thinking in the early years. *Thinking Skills and Creativity*, *1*(2), 108–119.

Csikszentmihalyi, M., (1991). *Flow: The Psychology of Optimal Experience*. London: Harper Collins.

Curtis, A., (1993). Play in different cultures and different childhoods. In Moyels, J. (Ed.), *The Excellence of Play*. Buckingham-Philadelphia: Open University Press.

Davidson, R. J., (1992). Anterior cerebral asymmetry and the nature of emotion. *Brain and Cognition*, *20*(1), 125–151.

Davies, D., (1999). *Child Development. A Practitioner's Guide*. New York: The Guildford Press.

De Luna, J. E., & Wang, D. C., (2021). Child traumatic stress and the sacred: Neurobiologically informed interventions for therapists and parents. *Religions*, *12*, 163. https://doi.org/10.3390/rel120 30163

Department for Education, (2015). Statutory Guidance Working Together to Safeguard Children. Available at: https://www.gov.uk/government/publications/working-together-to-safeguard-children–2 (Accessed 14 July 2022).

Department for Education (DfE), (2021). *Development Matters. Non-statutory Curriculum Guidance for the Early Years Foundation Stage*. Available at: https://assets.publishing.service.gov.uk/government/uploads/system/uploads/attachment_data/file/1007446/6.7534_DfE_Development_Matters_Report_and_illustrations_web__2_.pdf (Accessed 5 July 2023).

Department for Education, (2021). *Statutory Framework for the Early Years Foundation Stage*. Available at: https://www.gov.uk/government/publications/early-years-foundation-stage-framework–2 (Accessed 22 Nov 2021).

Dimitrova, N., & Moro, C., (2013). Common ground on object use associates with caregivers' gestures. *Infant Behavior and Development*, 36(4), 618–626. https://doi.org/10.1016/j.infbeh.2013.06.006

Doidge, N., (2007). *The Brain That Changes Itself: Stories of Personal Triumph from the Frontiers of Brain Science*. London: Penguin Books.

Doidge, N., (2015). *The brain's Way of Healing: Stories of Remarkable Recoveries and Discoveries*. London: Penguin.

Duncombe, R., & Preedy, P., (2018). Movement for learning. *Early Childhood Education Redefined* (pp. 48–60). London: Routledge.

Eager, D., & Little, H., (2014). Risk deficit disorder. In *Proceeding of IPWEA International Public Works Conference*. Available at: https://www.researchgate.net/profile/David_Eager/publication/266172540_RISK_DEFICIT_DISORDER/links/55bf3f0508ae092e96652b7c/RISK-DEFICIT-DISORDER.pdf (Accessed 16 Aug 2021).

Equality Act, (2010). [online] Available at: http://www.legislation.gov.uk/ukpga/2010/15/contents (Accessed 11 Jan 2015).

Erikson, E. H., (Ed.), (1963). *Youth: Change and Challenge*. New York: Basic Books.

Falk, S., Fasolo, M., Genovese, G., Romero-Lauro, L., & Franco, F., (2021). Sing for me, Mama! Infants' discrimination of novel vowels in song. *Infancy, 26*(2), 248–270.

Feldman, R., & Eidelman, A. I., (2007). Maternal postpartum behaviour and the emergence of infant-mother and infant-father synchrony in preterm and full-term infants. The role of neonatal vagal tone. *Developmental Psychobiology, 49*(3), 290–302.

Feldman, R., Magori-Cohen, R., Galili, G., Singer, M., & Louzoun, Y., (2011). Mother and infant coordinate heart rhythms through episodes of interaction synchrony. *Infant Behavior and Development, 34*(4), 569–577.

Field, T., (1985). Attachment as psychological attunement. In T. Field & M. Reite (Eds.), *The Psychobiology of Attachment and Separation*. New York: Academic Press.

Fisher, E. P., (1992). The impact of play on development: A meta-analysis. *Play & Culture, 5*(2), 159–181.

Fonagy, P., (2003). The development of psychopathology from infancy to adulthood: The mysterious unfolding of disturbance in time. *Infant Mental Health Journal, 24*(3), 212–239.

Franco, F., Suttora, C., Spinelli, M., Kozar, I., & Fasolo, M., (2021). Singing to infants matters: Early singing interactions affect musical preferences and facilitate vocabulary building. *Journal of Child Language, 49*(3), 552–577.

Franklin, A., Pitchford, N., Hart, L., Davies, I. R., Clausse, S., & Jennings, S., (2008). Salience of primary and secondary colours in infancy. *British Journal of Developmental Psychology, 26*(4), 471–483.

Fromkin, V., Krashen, S., Curtiss, S., Rigler, D., & Rigler, M., (1974). The development of language in genie: A case of language acquisition beyond the "critical period. *Brain and Language, 1*(1), 81–107.

Gallese, V., Eagle, M. N., & Migone, P., (2007). Intentional attunement: Mirror neurons and the neural under-pinnings of interpersonal relations. *Journal of the American Psychoanalytic Association, 55*(1), 131–175.

Geertz, C., (1973). *The Interpretation of Cultures*. New York: Basic Books.

Gerhardt, S., (2015). *Why Love Matters: How Affection Shapes a Baby's Brain*. London: Brunner-Routledge.

Gervais, M., & Wilson, D. S., (2005). The evolution and functions of laughter and humor: A synthetic approach. *The Quarterly Review of Biology, 80*(4), 395–430. https://doi.org/10.1086/498281

Gibson, J. L., Cornell, M., & Gill, T., (2017). A systematic review of research into the impact of loose parts play on children's cognitive, social and emotional development. *School Mental Health, 9*(4), 295–309.

Ginsburg, K. R., (2007). The importance of play in promoting healthy child development and maintaining strong parent-child bonds. *Pediatrics, 119*(1), 182–191.

Goldschmeid, E., & Jackson, S., (1994). *People under Three: Young Children in Day Care*. London: Routledge.

Goleman, D., (1998). *Working With Emotional Intelligence*. New York: Bantam Books.

Gopnik, A., Melzoff, A., & Kuhl, P., (1999). *How Babies Think: The Science of Childhood*. London: Weidenfeld and Nicolson.

Gordon, I., & Feldman, R., (2008). Synchrony in the triad: A microlevel process model of coparenting and parent-child interactions. *Family Process, 47*(4), 465–479.

Goswami, U., (2015). *Children's Cognitive Development and Learning*. Cambridge: Cambridge Primary Review Trust.

Gray, P., (2011). The decline of play and the rise of psychopathology in children and adolescents. *American Journal of Play, 3*(4), 443–463.

Greenfield, S., (2014). *Mind Change: How 21st Century Technology Is Leaving Its Mark on the Brain*. Random House.

Groos, K., (1901). *The Play of Man*. London: Heinemann.

Hadley, E., (2002). Playful disruptions. *Early Years: An International Journal of Research and Development*, 22(1), 9–17.

Hann, D. M., Osofsky, J. D., Barnard, K. E., & Leonard, G., (1994). Dyadic affect regulation in three caregiving environments. *American Journal of Orthopsychiatry*, 64, 263–269.

Hanson, R., (2013). *Hardwiring Happiness: The Practical Science of Reshaping Your Brain-and Your Life*. Random House.

Harding, J., (2015). *Children and Media: Developing a Tool for Analysis PHD*. Middlesex University (Embargoed).

Harding, J., (2022). Early years educator magazine, Volume 23, No. 11. *How Confident Are Parents in Managing Screen Time?* (pp. 31–33). London: Mark Allen Group.

Harding, J., (2019). Parents' lived experiences in the UK. *Young Consumers*, 20(2), 61–76.

Harding, J., & Chaudhuri, C., (2008). *Creative Wellbeing*. Basildon: Creative Partnerships.

Harding, J., & Meldon-Smith, L., (1999). *Play in Early Childhood: from Birth to Six Years*. London: Routledge.

Harris, P. L., (2000). *The Work of the Imagination*. Oxford: Blackwell.

Harrist, A. W., & Waugh, R. M., (2002). Dyadic synchrony: Its structure and function in children's development. *Developmental Review*, 22(4), 555–592.

Hart, B., & Risley, T., (2003). The early catastrophe: The 30 million word gap by age 3. *American Educator*, 27(4), 4–9.

Hassinger-Das, B., Hirsh-Pasek, K., & Golinkoff, R. M., (2017). The case of brain science and guided play. *Young Children*, 72(2), 45–50.

Hazen, E. P., Stornelli, J. L., O'Rourke, J. A., Koesterer, K., & McDougle, C. J., (2014). Sensory symptoms in autism spectrum disorders. *Harvard Review of Psychiatry*, 22, 112–124. https://doi.org/10.1097/01.hrp.0000445143.08773.58

Hewett, V. M., (2001). Examining the Reggio Emilia approach to early childhood education. *Early Childhood Education Journal*, 29(2), 95–100.

HM Government. (2015). *What to do If You're Worried a Child Is Being Abused: Advice for Practitioners*. [online] Available at: https://assets.publishing.service.gov.uk/government/uploads/system/uploads/attachment_data/file/419604/What_to_do_if_you_re_worried_a_child_is_being_abused.pdf (Accessed 1 June 2023).

HM Government. (2018). *Working Together to Safeguard Children: A Guide to Inter-Agency Working to Safeguard and Promote the Welfare of Children*. [online] Available at: https://assets.publishing.service.gov.uk/government/uploads/system/uploads/attachment_data/file/779401/Working_Together_to_Safeguard-Children.pdf (Accessed 17 April 2022).

Hosking, G., & Walsh, I., (2005). *The WAVE Report 2005: Violence and What to Do About It*. Croydon: WAVE Trust.

House of Commons Education Committee, (2019). *Tackling Disadvantage in the Early Years*. Available at: https://publications.parliament.uk/pa/cm201719/cmselect/cmeduc/1006/1006.pdf (Accessed 24 Aug 2022).

Hughes, B., (2012). *Evolutionary Playwork* (2nd ed.). London: Routledge.

Huizinga, J., (2014). *Homo ludens: A Study of the Play-Element in Culture*. London: Routledge.

Iacoboni, M., Woods, R. P., Brass, M., Bekkering, H., Mazziotta, J. C., & Rizzolatti, G., (1999). Cortical mechanisms of human imitation. *Science*, 286(5449), 2526–2528.

Isaacs, S., (1932). *The Social Development of Young Children. A Study of Beginnings*. London: Routledge and Kegan Paul.

Jambor, T., (2000). Informal, real-life play – Building children's brain connections. *Dimensions of Early Childhood*, *28*(4), 4–8.

Kaye, P., (2015). *The First Five Years Bath*. Bath: White Ladder Press.

Kim, M., (2002). Parents' perceptions and behaviors regarding toys for young children's play in Korea. *Education*, *122*(4).

Kress, G., (2003). *Literacy in the New Media Age*. London: Routledge.

Kuzawa, W., Chugani, C., Grossman, H., Lipovich, L., Muzik, L., Hof, O., Wildman, P., Sherwood, D., Leonard, C., & Lange, W., (2014). Metabolic costs and evolutionary implications of human brain development. *Proceedings of the National Academy of Sciences*, *111*(36), 13010–13015.

Laevers, F., (1994). *The Innovative Project Experiential Education and the Definition of Quality in Education. Studia Pedagogica*. Belgium: Leuven University Press.

Laible, D. J., & Thompson, R. A., (2000). Mother–child discourse, attachment security, shared positive affect, and early conscience development. *Child Development*, *71*(5), 1424–1440.

Landry, S. H., (1986). Preterm infants' responses in early joint attention interactions. *Infant Behavior and Development*, *9*(1), 1–14.

Lay, K. L., Waters, E., & Park, K. A., (1989). Maternal responsiveness and child compliance: The role of mood as a mediator. *Child Development*, *60*, 1405–1411.

Leslie, A. M., Friedman, O., & German, T. P., (2004). Core mechanisms in 'theory of mind'. *Trends in Cognitive Sciences*, *8*(12), 528–533.

Lewis, P., Boucher, J., Lupton, L., & Watson, S., (2000). Relationships between symbolic play, functional play, verbal and non-verbal ability in young children. *International Journal of Language and Communication Disorders*, *35*(1), 117–27.

Lillard, A. S., Lerner, M. D., Hopkins, E. J., Dore, R. A., Smith, E. D., & Palmquist, C. M., (2013). The impact of pretend play on children's development: A review of the evidence. *Psychological Bulletin*, *139*(1), 1.

Livingstone, S., Blum-Ross, A., & Zhang, D., (2018). *What Do Parents Think, and Do, about Their Children's Online Privacy?* Available at: http://eprints.lse.ac.uk/87954/1/Livingstone_Parenting%20Digital%20Survey%20Report%203_Published.pdf (Accessed 23 Aug 2022).

Marsh, J., (2010). Young children's play in online virtual worlds. *Journal of Early Childhood Research*, *8*(1), 23–39.

Marsh, J., & Bishop, J., (2013). *Changing Play: Play, Media and Commercial Culture from the 1950s to the Present Day*. Maidenhead: Open University Press.

Marsh, J., Brooks, G., Hughes, J., Ritchie, L., & Roberts, S., (2005). *Digital Beginnings: Young Children's Use of Popular Culture, Media and New Technologies*. Sheffield: University of Sheffield.

McEwen, B. S., & Lasley, E. N., (2005). *The End of Stress as We Know It*. New York: Henry Joseph Press.

Miller, G., Chen, E., & Parker, K., (2011). Psychological stress in childhood and susceptibility to the chronic diseases of aging. *Psychological Bulletin*, *137*(6), 959–997.

Mohandas, S., (2022). Beyond male recruitment: decolonising gender diversification efforts in the early years by attending to pastpresent material-discursive-affective entanglements. *Gender & Education*, *34*(1), 17–32. https://doi.org/10.1080/09540253.2021.1884202

Moore, C., & Dunham, P., (1995). *Joint Attention: Its Origins and Role in Development*. Hillsdale: Erlbaum.

Moro, C., & Rodríguez, C., (2005). *L'objet et la Construction de Son Usage chez le bébé. Une Approche Sémiotique du Développement Préverbal*. Bern: Peter Lang.

Moyles, J., (2010). *The Excellence of Play*. Maidenhead: Open University Press.

Mulligan, D. A., Ameenuddin, N., Brown, A., Christakis, D. A., Cross, C., Falik, H. L., Hill, D. L., & Hogan, M. J., (2012). The importance of play in promoting healthy child development and maintaining strong parent-child bond: Focus on children in poverty. *Pediatrics*, *129*(1), e204–e213.

Murnen, S. K., Greenfield, C., Younger, A., & Boyd, H., (2016). Boys act and girls appear: A content analysis of gender stereotypes associated with characters in children's popular culture. *Sex Roles*, *74*(1), 78–91.

Murray, L., & Trevarthen, C., (1986). The infant's role in mother–infant communications. *Journal of Child Language*, *13*(1), 15–29.

National Geographic, (2022). Washington, DC.

Nelson, C. A., Bhutta, Z. A., Harris, N. B., Danese, A., & Samara, M., (2020). Adversity in childhood is linked to mental and physical health throughout life. *British Medical Journal*, *371*. https://doi.org/10.1136/bmj.m3048

Ofcom, (2006). *Media Literacy Audit: Report on Media Literacy amongst Children*. Available at: https://www.ofcom.org.uk/research-and-data/media-literacy-research/childrens/children (Accessed 23 July 2022).

Ofcom, (2018). *Children and Parents: Media Use and Attitudes Report 2018*. Available at: https://www.ofcom.org.uk/research-and-data/media-literacy-research/childrens/children-and-parents-media-use-and-attitudes-report-2018 (Accessed 23 Aug 2022).

Ofcom, (2022). *Children and Parents: Media Use and Attitudes Report 2022*. Available at: https://www.ofcom.org.uk/research-and-data/media-literacy-research/childrens/children-and-parents-media-use-and-attitudes-report-2022 (Accessed 23 Aug 2022).

Ofsted, (2022). *Guidance for Early Years Inspection Handbook for Ofsted-Registered Provision*. Available at: https://www.gov.uk/government/publications/early-years-inspection-handbook-eif/early-years-inspection-handbook-for-ofsted-registered-provision-for-september-2021 (Accessed 14 Aug 2022).

Organisation for Economic Co-operation and Development (OECD), (2002). *Understanding the Brain towards a New Learning Science*. Paris: OECD Publishing.

Paley, V. G., (2004). *A Child's Work: The Importance of Fantasy Play*. University of Chicago Press.

Papadimitriou, A., Smyth, C., Politimou, N., Franco, F., & Stewart, L., (2021). The impact of the home musical environment on infants' language development. *Infant Behavior and Development*, *65*, 101651.

Parten, M. B., (1932). Social participation among preschool children. *Journal of Abnormal and Social Psychology*, *27*(3), 243–269.

Pellegrini, A. D., & Smith, P. K., (1998). Physical activity play: The nature and function of a neglected aspect of play. *Child Development*, *69*(3), 577–598. https://doi.org/10.2307/1132187

Piaget, J., (1936). *Origins of Intelligence in the Child*. London: Routledge and Kegan Paul.

Piaget, J., (1951). Principal factors determining intellectual evolution from childhood to adult life. *Organization and Pathology of Thought* (pp. 154–175). Columbia: Columbia University Press.

Preedy, P., Sanderson, K., & Ball, C. (eds.), (2018). *Early Childhood Education Redefined: Reflections and Recommendations on the Impact of Start Right*. London: Routledge.

Pyle, A., & Danniels, E., (2017). A continuum of play-based learning: The role of the teacher in play-based pedagogy and the fear of hijacking play. *Early Education and Development*, *28*(3), 274–289.

Qin, S., Young, C. B., Supekar, K., Uddin, L. Q., & Menon, V., (2012). Immature integration and segregation of emotion-related brain circuitry in young children. *Proceedings of the National Academy of Sciences*, *109*(20), 7941–7946.

Rideout, V. J., Vandewater, E. A., & Wartella, E. A., (2003). *Zero to Six: Electronic Media in the Lives of Infants, Toddlers and Preschoolers*. Washington: Kaiser.

Roberts, R., (2002). *Developing Self-Esteem in Young Children*. London: Paul Chapman/Sage.

Rushton, S., Juola-Rushton, A., & Larkin, E., (2010). Neuroscience, play and early childhood education: Connections, implications and assessment. *Early Childhood Education Journal*, 37(5), 351–361.

Sakr, M., (2019). *Digital Play in Early Childhood: What's the Problem?* London: Sage.

Sakr, M., Connelly, V., & Wild, M., (2018). Imitative or iconoclastic? How young children use ready-made images in digital art. *International Journal of Art and Design Education*, 37(1), 41–52.

Sanders, M. R., & Mazzucchelli, T. G., (2013). The promotion of self-regulation through parenting interventions. *Clinical Child and Family Psychology Review*, 16(1), 1–17.

Sapolsky, R. M., (2004). *Why Zebras Don't Get Ulcers*. New York: Times Books.

Selleck, D., & Griffin, S., (1996). Quality for the under threes. In G. Pugh (Ed.), *Contemporary Issues in the Early Years* (pp. 152–169) (2nd ed.). London: Paul Chapman/Sage.

Shaffer, D., (2009). *Social and Personality Development* (6th ed.). Wadsworth: Cengage Learning.

Shaffer, D. R., & Kipp, K., (2010). Developmental psychology. Childhood and Adolescence (9th Ed. International Edition). Wadsworth: Cengage Learning.

Shanker, S., & Hopkins, S., (2015). *Self-Regulation: A Discussion Paper for Goodstart Early Learning in Australia. Canada*: The Mehrit Centre Ltd.

Sheridan, M., (1977). *Spontaneous Play in Early Childhood: From Birth to Six Years* (1st ed.). Windsor: NFER.

Siegel, D., & Bryson, T. P., (2020). *The Power of Showing up: How Parental Presence Shapes Who Are Kids Become and How Their Brains Get Wired*. London: Scribe UK.

Siegel, D., & Bryson, T. P., (2012). *The Whole Brain Child: 12 Proven Strategies to Nurture Your Child's Developing Mind*. London: Robinson.

Sproule, L., Walsh, G., & McGuinness, C., (2019). More than 'just play': Picking out three dimensions of a balanced early years pedagogy. *International Journal of Early Years Education*, 27(4), 409–422. https://doi.org/10.1080/09669760.2019.1628011

Stern, D. N., (2004). *The Present Moment in Psychotherapy and Everyday Life*. WW Norton & Company.

Sternberg, R. J., & Powell, J. S., (1983). The development of intelligence. In P. H. Mussen (Ed.), *Handbook of Child Psychology* (4th ed., pp. 341–419). New York: John Wiley and Sons.

Stern, D. N., Hofer, L., Haft, W., & Dore, J., (1985). Affect attunement: The sharing of feeling states between mother and infant by means of intermodal fluency. In T. M. Field and N. A. Fox (Eds.), *Social Perception in Infants* (pp. 249–268) Norwood, NJ: Ablex.

Strong-Wilson, T., & Ellis, J., (2007). Children and place: Reggio Emilia's environment as third teacher. *Theory into Practice*, 46(1), 40–47.

Sturrock, G., Russell, W. and Else, P., (2004). Towards ludogogy: Parts I, II and III. *Oxford Therapeutic Playwork Association (2006). Therapeutic Playwork Reader Two 2000–2005* (pp. 60–95). Oxford: Oxford Playwork Association.

Sutton-Smith, B., (2001). *The Ambiguity of Play*. London: Harvard University Press.

Sutton-Smith, B., (2008). Play theory: A personal journey and new thoughts. *American Journal of Play*, 1(1), 80–123.

Tamis-LeMonda, C. S., Kuchirko, Y., & Song, L., (2014). Why is infant language learning facilitated by parental responsiveness? *Current Directions in Psychological Science*, 23(2), 121–126.

Ticktin, A., (2021). *Play to Progress*. London: Paitktus.

Tierney, A. L., & Nelson, C. A. III, (2009). Brain development and the role of experience in the early years. *Zero to Three*, 30(2), 9–13.

Tizard, B., & Harvey, D., (1977). *Biology of Play*. London: Spastics International Medical.

Tomasello, M., & Farrar, M. J., (1986). Joint attention and early language. *Child Development*, 57(6), 1454–1463.

Torrijos-Muelas, M., González-Víllora, S., & Bodoque-Osma, A. R., (2021). The persistence of neuromyths in the educational settings: A systematic review. *Frontiers in Psychology*, *11*, 591923. https://doi.org/10.3389/fpsyg.2020.591923

Trawick-Smith, J., Wolff, J., Koschel, M., & Vallarelli, J., (2014). Which toys promote high-quality play? Reflections on the five-year anniversary of the TIMPANI study. *YC Young Children*, 69(2), 40.

Trehub, S. E., Unyk, A. M., & Trainor, L. J., (1993). Maternal singing in cross-cultural perspective. *Infant Behavior and Development*, *16*(3), 285–295.

Trevarthen, C., (2008). The musical art of infant conversation: Narrating in the time of sympathetic experience, without rational interpretation, before words. Musicae Scientiae *Young Children*, 69, 40–47.

Tronick, E. Z., & Gianino, A., (1986). Interactive mismatch and repair: Challenges to the coping infant. *Zero to Three*, 6, 1–6.

Tsuk, K. E., (1998). *The Emotional Relationship between Mothers and Their Aggressive Young Children: An Observation of Mother–Child Interaction*. New York: York University.

Turkle, S., (2012). *Alone Together: Why We Expect More from Technologies and Less from Each Other*. New York: Basic Books.

United Nations Convention on the Rights of the Child, (1989). *United Nations, Treaty Series*, *1577*(3), 1–23.

Vanderschuren, L., (2010). How the brain makes play fun. *American Journal of Play*, *2*(3), 315–337.

Vanderschuren, L. J. M. J., & Trezza, V., (2014). What the laboratory rat has taught us about social play behavior: Role in behavioral development and neural mechanisms. *Current Topics in Behavioral Neurosciences*, *16*, 189–212.

Vecchi, V., (2010). *Art and Creativity in Reggio Emilia*. London: Routledge.

Vygotsky, L. S., & Cole, M., (1978). *Mind in Society: Development of Higher Psychological Processes*. Harvard University Press.

Walker, C. M., & Gopnik, A., (2013). *Pretense and Possibility – A Theoretical Proposal about the Effects of Pretend Play on Development*.

Wass, S. V., Noreika, V., Georgieva, S., Clackson, K., Brightman, L., Nutbrown, R., Covarrubias, L. S., & Leong, V., (2018). Parental neural responsivity to infants' visual attention: How mature brains influence immature brains during social interaction. *PLoS Biology*, *16*(12), e2006328.

White, J., (2019). *Playing and Learning Outdoors: The Practical Guide and Sourcebook for Excellence in Outdoor Provision and Practice with Young Children*. London: Routledge.

Whiting, A., & Williams, D., (2013). Why people use social media: A uses and gratifications approach. *Qualitative Market Research: An International Journal*, *16*(4), 362–369.

Winnicott, D. W., (1971). *Playing and Reality London. Tavistock Publications. Manuscript received September*, 22, p. 1993.

Winnicott, D. W., (1999). *Playing and Reality*. London: Routledge.

Winston, R., (2016). *All about Your Brain Big Questions*. London: DK Publishing.

World Health Organization, (2004). *The Importance of Caregiver-Child Interactions for the Survival and Healthy Development of Young Children: A Review*. Available at: https://apps.who.int/iris/bitstream/handle/10665/42878/924159134X.pdf

Index

NOTE: Pages in *italics* and **bold** refer to figures and tables, respectively.